Connections: A Relationship Based Phase Model

A MANUAL FOR EARLY CHILDHOOD PROFESSIONALS PROMOTING SOCIAL AND EMOTIONAL HEALTH IN YOUNG CHILDREN

By The Writing Group at the Virginia Frank Child Development Center,

Authored by Joni R. Crounse MA
with Kathy Ham LCSW
with Joanne Kestnbaum LCSW
with Wendy Guyer LCSW
with Linnet Mendez LCPC
with Laura Sheridan LCSW

Copyright © 2014 Authored by Joni R. Crounse MA
with Kathy Ham LCSW
with Joanne Kestnbaum LCSW
with Wendy Guyer LCSW
with Linnet Mendez LCPC
with Laura Sheridan LCSW

All rights reserved.

ISBN: 1497386802
ISBN 13: 9781497386808
Library of Congress Control Number: 2014903204
CreateSpace Independent Publishing Platform
North Charleston, South Carolina

To the children and families who inspire our work.

CONTENTS

Chapter 1 Overview of Connections: A Relationship-Based Phase Model — 1

Chapter 2 Phase One: Separation/Attachment — 7

Chapter 3 Phase Two: Autonomy — 27

Chapter 4 Phase Three: Initiative & Independence — 39

Chapter 5 Incorporating Morning Check-in into Your Classroom — 53

Chapter 6 Focus on Teachers — 63

Chapter 7 Parents — 75

Chapter 8 Relationship-Based Early Childhood Mental Health Consultation — 79

Chapter 9 Frequently Asked Questions — 85

Chapter 10 Theoretical Underpinnings — 89

Epilogue — 97

Acknowledgements — 105

PREFACE

Over the past fifty-nine years, the staff at Jewish Child and Family Services' Virginia Frank Child Development Center has used the Relationship-Based Phase Model to help preschool- and kindergarten-aged children who experience emotional, social, and behavioral challenges in the classroom. The staff is comprised of early childhood professionals with backgrounds in education, social work, child development, psychology, and counseling who provide direct services to children and families. The staff provides early childhood mental health consultation to daycares, preschools, and kindergarten programs in Chicago and its suburbs. This manual is intended for use in daycare and preschool settings. *Connections: A Relationship-Based Phase Model* is intended to complement programs that address children's unique social and emotional needs within the framework of group formation and relationships that develop over a year's time.

We propose that early childhood professionals who are attuned to the emotional and environmental contexts of children's lives are able to meet best practice standards. *Connections: A Relationship-Based Phase Model* provides practical tools to help caregivers address the social and emotional needs of young children in order to promote a solid foundation for learning.

Early childhood professionals know that children's social-emotional needs change over the course of the program year and that patterns of behavior are evident. The intent of *Connections* is to examine those patterns of behavior and to understand them in a developmental and relational framework. Along with this, *Connections* details concrete techniques to respond to these patterns of behavior in a developmentally appropriate way.

Early Childhood Mental Health Consultants from Jewish Child & Family Services' Virginia Frank Child Development Center have helped early childhood teachers, directors, and caregivers to incorporate the Relationship-Based Phase Model into the curricula of their centers with the aim of increasing awareness and improving responses to children's social and emotional needs in the classroom. This past fiscal year, FY14, 84% of directors and 97% of teachers across fifteen consultation sites reported that Mental Health Consultants increased administrators' and teachers' understanding of children's social/emotional and developmental functioning across phases of the year.

Connections will help caregivers and teachers develop strategies for managing the powerful emotions that children evoke in them. Teachers will develop skills for talking about the children's emotions as well as their own. These skills will allow caregivers and teachers to assist children in coping with a wide range of emotions and behavioral responses to the challenges of everyday life in the classroom. *Connections* includes interactive examples and strategies based on familiar situations that arise in the classroom setting. Those of us in the field of early childhood mental health understand that secure attachments are the basis for healthy relationships throughout one's lifespan and optimal cognitive growth and development. In other words: CONNECTIONS!

References

Atwool, N. 1997. "Attachment as a Context for Development: Challenges and Issues." *Children's Issues Seminar*. University of Otago, New Zealand.

Stern, D. 1985. *The Interpersonal World of the Infant*. New York: Basic Books.

Yalom, I. 1995. *The Theory and Practice of Group Development*. New York: Basic Books.

CHAPTER 1

Overview Of *Connections: A Relationship-Based Phase Model*

IT'S ALL ABOUT THE CONNECTIONS: A BRIEF OVERVIEW OF THE MODEL

> *The Relationship-Based Phase Model* will give you a framework to understand how the social-emotional world of young children evolves over the rhythm of the school year.

Connections: *The Relationship-Based Phase Model* will give you a framework to understand how the social-emotional world of young children evolves over the rhythm of the school year. Learning this model will help you take a step back and make sense of the bigger picture of how relationships affect learning in preschool-age children. *Connections: The Relationship-Based Phase Model* divides the year into three periods that are roughly equal. This model can be used with either a year-round or a school-year-based program, regardless of whether children are with you for a whole or half-day. It is applicable to preschool programs where the children range in age from two to six years. Elements of this model can be adapted to other types of programs, such as camps or afterschool programs, as well. In the fall, in Phase One, the focus is on separation from family and creating a secure attachment to the teachers, mirroring the earliest phases of child development (Siegel and Hartzell 2003). In Phase Two, in the middle of the year, children are gaining a sense of independence, and the activities, songs, and books will support their capacity for autonomy. You may recognize this phase as the time of year when you as a teacher begin to feel annoyed or downright aggravated, as well as depleted by the demands of the group. During Phase Three, in the last part of the program year, you notice that children are able to act more independently and take increasing initiative. Children consolidate the skills and relationships that have been shaped throughout the year. This is the time of year when you can sit back and say, "Wow, look at all they can do!" You know this happens, but why? How can you promote the children's mastery in this context of change throughout a typical school year? How do you promote attachment with entering children and help children who are saying good-bye and moving on to kindergarten?

Connections: The Relationship-Based Phase Model recognizes that young children develop best in the context of secure relationships. The fundamentals of all relationships mirror the first three years of life, when the child progresses through the phases of trust, autonomy, and initiative/independence (Erikson 1963). You can see this in your classroom when children enter for the first time. You notice how each child approaches you and the other children, as well as how he or she handles the separation from the caregiver. Some children cling, others protest and scream, many sob, and some seem not to notice when parents leave. You start to realize with experience that the children's styles of separating from their caregivers and greeting you from the first moment are often echoed in the ways they establish relationships in the classroom. Children may come in with emotional challenges, having experienced insecurity before. Experiences such as a move to a new home, loss of a loved one, divorce, or violence in their community all have a great impact on how these children behave in your classrooms (Lieberman and Van Horn 2008). Children with challenging experiences often worry more about whether you as a teacher can keep them safe and provide for them. They may have less energy to devote to learning than children who are more secure in relationships. Structure, consistency in relationships, clear limits, and simple routines can reassure these children that the classroom will be safe and predictable. You also become an important support so that their development will not be derailed.

Connections: The Relationship-Based Phase Model can be combined with the curriculum you are already using in your classroom to enhance your understanding of the process of moving from attachment toward independence

> **Connections: The Relationship-Based Phase Model recognizes that young children develop best in the context of secure relationships.**

in the normal course of a school year. All classrooms are alive with group dynamics (Koplow 1996). In many professions, but especially in the emotionally driven world of young children, group dynamics play a huge part in how we experience our day. If things are flowing well and lines of communication with coworkers and parents are open, then we find that children are often more secure, more easily soothed, and act out less. Why is this? If we as professional caregivers and teachers can feel secure that we will be heard, understood, and responded to in ways that meet our needs a good portion of the time, we will be calmer and more open to others. The same is true for the children (Siegel and Hartzell 2003). If either we or the children are constantly feeling that our needs cannot be met, we get agitated and can start to show signs of stress that affect each other and the group as a whole (Goldstein 1995).

As the year flows from a focus on attachment toward children's developing more autonomy and initiative, we recognize that the year also flows from children at first trying to get their individual needs met to children gradually developing a sense of group identity. At first, it might not matter so much to some children that they are part of your school or a particular group, but by the end of the year, most children proudly identify what school they attend and are happy to announce to people they know that they are in a group. This sense of belonging happens as a process over the course of the year and must start with teachers' encouraging all children's membership in the group (Yalom 1995).

As the school year progresses, children's behaviors change. As a childcare provider, you are aware that separation is more challenging at the beginning of the school year. Children will have an easier time leaving their parents as their attachment to you develops. When children have secure relationships with caregivers, they have the capacity to be more socially competent (Sameroff and Emde 1989). What is typical at the beginning of the year for most of the children in your classroom might signal a problem for a particular child later in the year. An example of this would be a child who cries at drop-off every day and clings to his or her parent. This is expected in Phase One, but by Phase Three, we would start to wonder why the child is demonstrating a high level of distress at separating. Throughout the year, we keep in mind that all behavior has meaning and communicates to us, as caregivers, how a child or a group of children is feeling. As you progress through *Connections*, you will develop more awareness of the underlying meaning of

> Children will have an easier time leaving their parents as their attachment to you develops.

children's behaviors. *Connections* also addresses how to respond to children whose behaviors are atypical and suggests changes in the classroom that may help. In addition, this manual details interventions as assessments that might be needed for more serious behavioral issues.

Figure 1 provides you with a visual of the three phases and the six aspects of each phase of the Connections model. The following chapters explain these phases in depth.

Overview Of Connections: A Relationship-Based Phase Model

VIRGINIA FRANK CHILD DEVELOPMENT CENTER'S "CONNECTIONS: A RELATIONSHIP-BASED PHASE MODEL"

	Separation/Attachment Phase One	Autonomy Phase Two	Initiative & Independence Phase Three
Developmental Focus	• First steps in mastering separation anxiety • Ability to hold onto image of parent • Develop trust in teacher • Find comfort and sense of belonging within classroom setting – emotional & physical needs	• Sense of independent self • Go away/come back • Testing strength of relationship with teacher/trust • Emerging focus on peer relationships, including competition	• Develop initiative • Internalize rules • "Saying good-bye" • Gender identification through play and talk
Typical Behaviors	• Anxiety • Clinginess • Tearfulness • Agitation • Quiet • Difficulty sharing	• "I can do it myself." • Oppositional behavior • Limit testing • Experimentation • Asserting individual preferences	• Developing new skills/competencies • Identification with the group • Anxiety about endings
Teacher Responses	• Self awareness • Calm & soothing • Focus on developing nurturing relationships • Verbalizing and accepting children's feelings while maintaining limits	• Self-awareness (authenticity) • Holding structure • Clear expectations stated ahead of time • Sense of humor • Recognizing group contagion • Balance between holding on and letting go	• Self awareness • Encourage group interaction • Facilitating group problem solving • Feelings
Routines	• Simple and predictable • Few and clear transitions • Less time in large group (subgrouping) • Importance of initial free play • Providing for children	• Develop large group activities • Greater focus on sharing and waiting • Jobs • Sub-grouping • Community	• More flexibility • Changes in schedule to accommodate larger explorations/projects • Field trips • Practice separation within school
Environment	• Uncluttered • Safe • Limiting choices	• Provide emotional and physical space for moving away from teacher • Give more choices • Provide product-orientated activities and skill-building opportunities • Give firm but flexible structure	• Allow for children to "reconstruct" space • Expand "classroom" space (hallways and other parts of building)
Curriculum Presentation	• Simple, concrete, one day projects • Not focus on sharing • Individual set up • Focus on exploring materials • Sensory materials	• More complicated projects • More choices – open ended projects • Activities promoting experimentation – messiness • Group activities requiring more turn taking, waiting	• Include group creative experiences – plays • Group art projects, murals • Include child initiated curricular ideas • Creating books reviewing the year, anticipating future

Fig. 1: Connections: The Relationship-Based Phase Model

References

Erikson, E. H. 1963. *Childhood and Society*. New York: Norton.

Goldstein, E. 1995. *Ego Psychology and Social Work Practice*. New York: The Free Press.

Koplow, L. 1996. *Unsmiling Faces: How Preschools Can Heal*. New York: Teachers College Press.

Lieberman, A. and P. Van Horn. 2008. *Psychotherapy with Infants and Young Children: Repairing the Effects of Stress and Trauma on Early Attachment*. New York: Guilford Press.

Sameroff, A. and R. Emde, Eds. 1989. *Relationship Disturbances in Early Childhood: A Developmental Approach*. New York: Basic Books.

Seigel, D. and M. Hartzell. 2003. *Parenting from the Inside Out: How a Deeper Self-understanding Can Help You Raise Children Who Thrive*. New York: Penguin Putnam, Inc.

Winnicott, D. W. 1965. *The Maturational Processes and the Facilitating Environment*. London: Karnac.

Yalom, I. 1995. *The Theory and Practice of Group Therapy*. New York: Basic Books.

CHAPTER 2

Phase One
SEPARATION/ ATTACHMENT

> **The goal of Phase One is to help children separate from their caregivers and make secure relationships with their teachers.**

The goal of Phase One of the Relationship-Based Model is to help children separate from their caregivers and make secure relationships with the teachers. We come into a new school year with hope, excitement, and a lot of unknowns. In this jumble of energy, the work you do in the beginning that makes order out of chaos will set the stage for an organized classroom where you and the children can focus on learning. When children master a routine and schedule, they feel safe and good about themselves. That good feeling will help them be available to learn new tasks over the course of the year. We like to think of the motto for this beginning phase of getting to know or reconnecting with children as "less is more." What we mean by "less is more" is that the most fundamental connection children will make with important people in their lives comes from knowing and developing trust over time. Our goal in teaching the fundamentals of the Relationship-Based Phase Model is to help teachers tune into children's emotional needs and to lay the foundation for social relationships. It helps for teachers to take the child's perspective. Imagine being the size of a three-year-old and walking into the classroom for the first time. Even without the other children, we imagine that a new classroom is exciting for some and perhaps frighteningly large to others. How can we make the classroom a child-sized world in which all children feel comfortable?

Connections: A Relationship-Based Phase Model

Some of the children entering your program in the fall will be coming for the first time, and others will be returning after a break. New children don't know the rules and expectations in a classroom, and returning children may have forgotten them. The class is a new group, and everyone needs time to get used to one another. Though the beginning of the year may feel disjointed, critical emotional learning is taking place that will lay the foundations for ongoing learning.

Phase One sets the tone for the whole year. During this time the focus is on building relationships with children and parents. It's a critical period when children learn to feel safe and secure in their new environment so that they can learn and thrive in a group setting.

ATTACHMENT IS DEFINED AS

an emotional bond between an infant or toddler and primary caregiver, a strong bond being vital for the child's normal behavioral and social development.
(Dictionary.com)

Can you think of a beginning-of-the-year example of this in your classroom?

Developmental Focus: Separation/Attachment—It's All about Trust and Comfort

Throughout Phase One and beyond, teachers and staff work together as providers of:

- Nurturance
- Protection
- Consistency in relationships
- An alliance with family
- Comfort, calm, and soothing
- Anticipation of needs

Children's first task in a new school year is to separate with minimal stress from their parents and attach to their teacher. The goal is for children to find comfort and a sense of belonging within their new classroom setting. This can be accomplished through the teacher's ability to be responsive to children's emotional and physical needs. Children need assurances that although their parents will go away, they will come back for them. This assurance comes when children develop the ability to "hold onto" the idea of their parents. When children hold onto the idea of their parents, they are thinking about them and are able to have a basic trust that their parents love them and will remember them, too. They need to trust that their parents will return at the end of the day and that teachers will meet their needs throughout the day until they are reunited with their parents.

WHAT YOU MIGHT WORRY ABOUT:

Some teachers worry that talking about parents will make the children more worried. Usually children are already playing or acting out their insecurities. It helps for you to give them words to validate their fears of separation and abandonment and assure them that their parents are returning.

During the preschool years, children do not yet understand the complex world of feelings and motivations. They need assurances that their parents will go away and come back to them. Tell them the truth: "Mommy is going to work and will pick you up at the end of the day." If children are not given the truth, their fantasies can make them more anxious. You as a teacher can create a safe place in the classroom to give voice to these fears and to soothe children. You begin to foster a sense that the classroom is a community where children can connect around common feelings and shared experiences. As the year progresses, children will begin to use each other, but at the beginning they need you to create an open and accepting dialogue.

TYPICAL BEHAVIORS: ALL BEHAVIOR HAS MEANING

- Anxiety
- Clinginess to parents and teachers
- Agitation
- Shyness
- Quiet
- Resistance to transitions
- Defiance
- Crying
- Difficulty being soothed
- Hesitancy in sharing toys and teachers' attention

While children are attempting to master separating from parents and attaching to you during Phase One, they might exhibit some of the behaviors listed on the previous page. Children do not yet trust that their needs will be met. It is important to remember that all behavior has meaning.

You might notice that some children have not yet developed the language to express their needs and fears in the same way that many adults can. This means having to decode the meaning of child behaviors, and it can be very stressful to try to do this in the busy classroom. Often, children regress and lose the words for emotions during stress; they need you to help them calm down and regain regulation and control.

Why Is It Important to Talk about Feelings with the Group?
When a child cries, you might be hesitant to talk to him or her about missing parents because you fear that other children might hear this and also start crying. It's hard when there is a lot of sadness or anger being passed around the room. If you can begin the dialogue about feelings, you'll find that other children will be soothed by watching you validate another child's feelings. Why is this? Ultimately, these types of interactions help children regain emotional equilibrium, allowing them to feel more relaxed and less anxious. Children (and adults!) are comforted when you hear their underlying communication. They feel understood and trust that you are available to help them make sense of overwhelming feelings. Take the case of Emmie:

> *Emmie (four years old) is sitting in her locker trying to put on her shoes for outside time. She somehow shoves her left shoe onto her right foot. She looks up. Her teacher is helping another child zip his sweater. All of a sudden Emmie stands up and cries loudly, "Ow!" This gets her teacher's attention! She says, "Are you OK, Emmie?" Through her tears, Emmie points to her feet. Her teacher notices Emmie's shoe and says, "Oh, let me help you. I see why you said 'Ow!' It's on the wrong foot."*

Emmie's dilemma is typical of an interaction in Phase One. Emmie wants her shoe on, and normally her mother would do this for her. She is hesitant to ask the teacher for help because she doesn't know the teacher well and the teacher is busy helping another child. Emmie finds a way to get her teacher's attention by crying, and the teacher immediately reads Emmie's cues of distress to figure out why she is upset. In helping Emmie with this simple task, the teacher shows that she will understand and be able to care for Emmie when she falters. This helps Emmie build trust in the teacher and the classroom.

IN PHASE ONE, TEACHERS AND STAFF HELP CHILDREN AND PARENTS TO…

- Develop trust
- Separate from each other
- Master initial anxiety
- Relax and find comfort
- Feel a sense of belonging in the classroom
- Feel accepted and valued as individuals within the classroom group
- Build good relationships with teachers and staff

Phase One SEPARATION/ATTACHMENT   13

In Phase One, the beginnings and endings of school days are important transition times for children and parents alike and often are emotionally charged. Children feel secure when they trust that their teachers and caregivers are working together as they enter a new school environment or return from a break. Teachers who greet parents and engage in brief and casual conversations can get to know them. Parents are a teacher's best ally and an invaluable resource in getting to know a child. Building this relationship with parents can help teachers feel more connected to children early on by getting to know children through their parents' eyes. Parents feel more secure when their first experience of a teacher is positive and relaxed, and the more comfortable a parent is, the more comfortable a child will be when separating and transitioning into the classroom. During pick-up and drop-off times, it is important for teachers to save more in-depth conversations about problems or concerns for a private meeting or phone call, as this might heighten children's worries and make parents feel exposed. When parents and teachers are of different cultures or have conflicting beliefs about child rearing, teachers who attempt to understand parents' perspectives can provide more of a bridge to children who might react to the confusion. Teachers and parents can partner to educate each other about what the children experience at home and in school. The relationship between parents and teachers provides the foundation for collaboration when difficulties arise with children. As teachers get to know parents, they will become more attuned to stresses that may impact children's abilities to manage themselves in the classroom and learn. We discuss this further in Chapter 7, Parents.

TEACHERS RESPONSES: A BALANCING ACT
- Self-awareness
- Calm and soothing
- Focus on developing and nurturing relationships
- Verbalize and accept children's feelings while maintaining limits

In Phase One, your first task is to provide trust, comfort, and protection for children. You are trying to help children learn that they can depend on you, their teachers, to make sense of their new classroom. Remember, in Phase One, *less is more*. What does this mean? Children will feel nurtured and comforted by teachers who have a calm demeanor and a soothing tone of voice. This means building in less demanding activities and more time for observing and being available to children. Your focus should be broad. You will need to be aware of the different ways that children interact with you, others, and the toys and materials. Here's an example:

> *Six children are seated at the play dough table, each with an adequate amount of play dough. There are only four extruders and three rolling pins. You notice that Jimmy has taken all of the extruders and rolling pins and place them next to him. Suzie is whining, "I don't have any. He took them all!" The other four children begin whining, too.*

WATCH AND WONDER: QUESTIONS TO ASK
- Why did Jimmy take all of the play dough toys?
- Why is Suzie upset?
- Why did the other children begin whining?
- What should I do about it?

We're glad you asked! First, with a calm demeanor, ask Jimmy why he needed all the play dough toys. Jimmy might not be able to give you a verbal response, but he might tear up. Then you might say to him, "I wonder if you were worried that you might not have enough?" Jimmy is likely to look at you and nod his head. You might now say, "I see there isn't enough for everyone to have their own. I can fix that." Sharing is hard in Phase One. The ability to share will evolve as children trust they have enough. Jimmy's need to have all the toys triggered the other children's feelings of not having enough. With our response to Jimmy, the other children were soothed.

Remember that the goal in Phase One is attachment. You achieve attachment by doing things for children that they might normally be able to do for themselves. Recall the example of Emmie and her shoes. You might worry that this type of help will create dependence or undermine a child's ability to learn new skills. However, there will be plenty of time for that in a short while once children are settled into the program and comfortable. It is true that children will need skills in living through disappointments without falling apart, but in the beginning it helps to avoid overwhelming disappointments. Without an adult's help in working through things, children can feel lost and express their feelings in ways that get immediate—and often negative—attention. In time, you can help them gradually be able to handle more frustration. Tying children's shoes or helping them take off their coats, even if they are able to do these things on their own already, can promote trust that will enable them to feel more secure when trying new things in a few short weeks. We are always aware of the principle that young children learn best when adults first give them help in things and then gradually allow for more and more independence.

Throughout the Phases, being tuned into your own feelings and emotional responses to children's behaviors will be important. Working with young children often evokes strong emotions and reactions in us that can make this work quite rewarding and also quite challenging. You may find that children's behaviors can trigger your own feelings about how you were raised or how you are raising your own children. There are always differences between your culture or your family's rules and expectations and those of the children in your classroom. The following vignette illustrates how children may have different cultural backgrounds from teachers.

In a classroom the teacher sees that three-year-old Esme cries inconsolably on her cot during naptime. The teacher knows Esme is exhausted. She is at school at the crack of dawn and plays all morning. Her parents don't seem to understand that it's a long day for her. She needs to rest. The teacher finally learns from Esme's mother that at home Esme sleeps in the same bed as her two sisters. The teacher thinks that co-sleeping is harmful to children, as it does not help them settle and fall asleep independently. But with some help from her supervisor, the teacher recognizes her own cultural biases and finds a way to be near Esme at the beginning of naps to help settle her.

In this example, the teacher used supervision to understand the child's experience and to bridge between the cultures of home and classroom. The teacher can use this information to problem-solve with Esme's family to help her sleep at school during naptime.

Getting to Your Calm and Soothing Place

When we step back and reflect on our responses to children's behaviors, we are better able to meet a child's emotional needs in a way that promotes attachment with us as teachers. How does this work? Let's examine an example. A child who has a hard time separating from his parent at drop-off might lash out at a teacher. Even though the child is lashing out toward the teacher, this behavior is often more about distress at separating from a parent and transitioning from home to school. Most likely, the child really likes his teachers but still feels sad and angry at having to say good-bye to his parent. If a teacher can speak to this child's distress by saying something simple such as, "I know it's hard to say good-bye to Mommy, but I'm not going to let you hit me. I am going to help you take off your coat and go to circle time. Mommy comes back at the end of the day." The child will be soothed knowing that the teacher can tune into the feelings underlying his behavior. Children are comforted by knowing that despite difficult emotions, the teacher will still be available to meet their basic needs. An important role for you in Phase One is to verbalize and accept children's underlying feelings while helping them stop aggressive or destructive behaviors. Pairing limits and emotional attunement is a powerful way to help children be soothed and comforted. This is how you promote nurturing relationships and strong attachments.

> **Limits and emotional attunement promote nurturing relationships and strong attachements.**

Limits Make Children Feel Safe

Setting boundaries gives children clear ideas of what limits are and helps them feel safe. Children in Phase One need to know what is expected of them. It is important for you to maintain and follow through on the limits you set so that children learn that teachers' rules have meaning. This can be quite a challenge in a place where multiple children may be pushing limits at once. When you set limits, use a calm, clear, and firm voice. Whenever possible use natural consequences. If a child throws a truck, for example, and you've said that toys will be put away if thrown, you have to follow through and take the truck away. The children in the class will know and understand what the expectations are for their behavior. Children feel secure when they know what to expect, and this consistency helps them trust us. Children learn self-control when adults repeatedly set clear and consistent limits. They gradually internalize these limits and gain self-control.

ROUTINES: KEEP IT SIMPLE AND PREDICTABLE
- Simple and predictable
- Few and clear transitions
- Less time in large groups
- Importance of initial free play with limited choices
- Providing for children

As a new teacher, I walked into my classroom on my first day. The schedule for the day was hanging behind a shelf, where teachers could see it but children could not. The schedule was different each day, as different classrooms needed to share the gross-motor space. I stared at the schedule and realized that I could not hold it in my own head and wondered how the children would be able to do so. The classroom, while organized into different areas such as block play, was not labeled as such, and it was hard to tell where the boundaries lay. If I was this confused, I wondered how the children would know where to be at different times of day. I wondered if I could do something to change this. I worked with my co-teacher and together we made a new schedule with pictures and times that we featured on our story rug where we and the children could point to it. This structure helped us feel organized, and it gave us the tools to help children get through the day in an organized way.

Routines provide children and teachers with a predictable and consistent plan for each day and are particularly important in Phase One. You are responsible for developing routines, and children initially rely on you to guide them throughout the day. This helps organize the classroom and helps children internalize a sense of what to expect. Use a visual schedule that is at the children's eye level. Verbally go over the routine at the beginning of each day to help children gain a sense of what will happen.

EXAMPLE SCHEDULE

- Reading
- Free play
- Clean up
- Snack (breakfast)
- Circle time
- Center time (Choice time)
- Outside time
- Toileting and washing
- Lunch
- Toilet
- Nap time
- End of day

Children are calmer and feel more in control when they can predict what will happen next. It helps to keep the routine as consistent as possible over the course of the school year and to inform children when changes to the routine will happen. Children who experience routines have an easier time waiting, delaying gratification, and feeling calm during transitions. Transitions and waiting can be difficult for many children. The fewer transitions the better for young children. During Phase One, less is more.

TIPS TO ALLEVIATE STRESS DURING TRANSITIONS:

- Prepare children for transitions by saying, "In five minutes…"
- Whenever possible, sing about the transition. Be creative and make up a tune.
- Using a timer or flicking the lights to signal a transition can help.
- Narrate where the group is and what's coming next.
- Gain children's attention before moving on, such as by saying, "Eyes on me!"

Remember, we all need to know where to be and at what time or what's expected of us!

Beginning the day with a free playtime can provide a nice transition from home to school, and it also gives teachers an opportunity to gauge children's moods and connect with them in a relaxed manner. Free play is a natural way for children to express themselves, learn how to problem solve, develop and act out their ideas, develop friendships, express natural curiosity about the classroom and people in it, and more. Building in more opportunities for free play, while still maintaining clear structure, is less stressful than playing collaborative games. During Phase One, children have not developed the skills to negotiate these games effectively and can get overwhelmed. Often, it helps to divide children into smaller groups or subgroups in order for children and teachers to get to know each other better at the beginning of Phase One.

During Phase One, the routine should include ample opportunities for teachers to nurture children. At this stage, it is more important for children to develop a healthy relationship with teachers than with each other. Once children develop a secure attachment to teachers, teachers can help children get to know each other and play together. In the beginning of the program year, teachers can promote children's attachment by doing more for children, rather than by delegating jobs to them. Trust in the teacher, coupled with knowledge of the routine, helps children feel comfortable in the school environment. And this in turn helps children be more ready to learn and socialize with peers.

A WORD ON SUBGROUPING: YOU MIGHT, FOR EXAMPLE, HAVE A GROUP OF CHILDREN IN FREE PLAY WHILE ANOTHER GROUP WORKS THE ART TABLE.

When to do it:

- At initial circle time
- At snack time
- At meal time
- At choice time
- At story time

Why to do it:

- Minimizes stimulation
- Reduces distraction
- Promotes teacher-child attachment
- Provides more opportunities for eye contact
- Allows for dialogue with less competition

Classroom Environment: Less Is More

A classroom environment should:

- Focus on children and teachers
- Focus on process, not product
- Reduce stimulation
- Be simple and predictable
- Have clearly defined boundaries
- Be structured for comfort
- Establish routines
- Be teacher directed
- Have limited choices

During Phase One, the focus is on the relationship between the teachers and the children. Projects are less important at this time of the year. It is important to have the walls and surfaces clean and clear. Having less in the environment makes it easier for teachers to develop and maintain eye contact, reciprocity, and connection because children are less distracted by objects and artwork. Teachers are able to look at and reach a child in distress, if needed. Teachers can construct an environment that will provide for a range of individual needs in a group setting that meshes with early childhood developmental best practices. An environment with limited amounts of stimulation, clear boundaries, and predictability is soothing. During Phase One, children will respond well to limited choices in toys and activities and will look to you to guide play and small-group activities.

Activities that Enhance Your Curriculum: Process not Product

Being available to the children and getting to know them is the key to Phase One activities. Children must feel safe and well cared for in order to develop academic skills. In Phase One, activities should be kept simple.

WHY TO DO IT:
- It facilitates the children focusing on the teacher and each other
- It allows the teacher to check in with each child's emotional state (this will be addressed in Chapter 5 Incorporating Morning Check-in into Your Classroom)
- It reduces anxiety around competition
- It allows for exploration of play materials rather than coming up with original ideas
- It facilitates the teacher's capacity to assess play skills

HOW TO DO IT:
- Preparation in Phase One is paramount; have your materials ready
- Keep the activities simple
- Make the activities safe
- Use individual bins or trays for materials, as sharing is challenging at this time
- Have clearly defined steps
- Limit choices

Phase One Activities

Activity time during Phase One is structured to be simple and safe and to have clearly defined steps that lead to successful completion. This facilitates the children's focus on each other and the teacher.

Example sensory activities:
- Play dough (individual trays—cookie cutters, rollers, toys to push into the play dough)
- Water (individual bins—dolls, washcloths, sponges, soap, cups, etc.; add as you go along)
- Sand (individual bins—simple toys)
- Soap bubbles (individual cup and straws)
- Simple cooking (pudding, frosting graham crackers)
- Simple manipulatives
- Legos or Duplos
- Large beads with patterns
- Parquetry blocks with patterns
- Pegboards (simple patterns)

Example art activities:
- Watercolors (pre-drawn simple pictures to color in if your program allows)
- Coloring (pre-drawn pictures)
- Easel painting (pre-drawn pictures with one or two colors)
- Individual maps (home–school–home)
- Stickers (pre-drawn grids for structure and background pictures)
- Cut-and-paste simple precut patterns or pictures of faces, foods from magazines, or family, school, or school buses
- Paper chains
- Tissue paper collages
- Calendars or placemats

Example free-play activities:
- Simple dress-up clothes with limited choices
- Baby dolls, diapers, bottles, and carriages

- Kitchen area with limited food items and dishes
- Play telephones
- Doll houses

Phase One Books

The books used during Phase One are usually short, do not demand a long attention span, and focus on themes that are appropriate to this phase. These themes include attachment, separation, nurturance, caregiving, belongingness, and awareness of a separate self. The books range from simple fantasy stories to very concrete events similar to what the children are experiencing, such as a preschool child's first school experience. The following are good examples:

- Aliki, *Hello! Good-bye!*
- Margaret Wise Brown, *Angus and the Ducks*
- Margaret Wise Brown, *Goodnight Moon*
- Eric Carle, *Brown Bear, Brown Bear*
- Eric Carle, *The Very Hungry Caterpillar*
- Miriam Cohen, *Will I Have a Friend?*
- P. D. Eastman, *Are You My Mother?*
- Don Freeman, *Corduroy*
- Eric Hill, *Where's Spot?* (series)
- Holly Keller, *What Alvin Wanted*
- Marisabina, *Where Is Ben?*
- Robert McCloskey, *Blueberries for Sal*
- Emmy Payne, *Katy No-Pocket*
- Audrey Penn, *The Kissing Hand*
- Eve Rice, *Sam Who Never Forgets*
- Harlow Rockwell, *My Nursery School*
- Ann Herbert Scott, *On Mother's Lap*
- Anna Dewdney, *Llama Llama Misses Mama*
- Simple nursery rhymes

Phase One Songs

Phase One songs are designed to be low-key and soothing. Music time should be adult-centered and offer the children lots of repetition and predictability. Typical songs focus on identifying oneself and each other, one's own body parts, and where children's bodies are in space. They also focus on current tasks, such as riding the bus, separations, and reunions. Examples include:

- "Hello and How Are You?"
- "Five Little Ducks"
- "Sticky, Sticky, Sticky Bubblegum"
- "Open Shut Them"
- "The Wheels on the Bus"
- "If You're Happy and You Know It"
- "Little Fish"
- "Twinkle, Twinkle Little Star"
- "Head, Shoulders, Knees, and Toes"

Phase One Conclusion

The theme of Phase One is setting a framework for promoting children's development by building strong relationships. This phase focuses on children's need to trust their teachers. If you do a good job building relationships, by the end of this phase around winter break, children will feel secure in their environment and be open and available to the more complex learning that you will introduce in Phase Two. While we offer suggestions for specific activities, songs, and books that promote the themes of attachment and getting to know each other, we hope that you have gained a sense that your presence and your emotional tone are most important in helping children to transition to a new program year. This doesn't mean that you have to be perfect; it is enough to be a "good-enough" teacher (Winnicott 1958). Teachers go through transitions too, and in Chapter 6 we talk more about support for you.

References

Balaban, Nancy. 2006. *Everyday Goodbyes*. New York: Teachers College Press.

Greenspan, Stanley. 2000. *Building Healthy Minds: The Six Experiences That Create Intelligence and Emotional Growth in Babies and Young Children*. Boston: Da Capo Press.

Stern, Daniel N. 1985. *The Interpersonal World of the Infant*. New York: Basic Books.
Winnicott, D. W. 1958. *Collected Papers: Through Paediatrics to Psycho-analysis*. New York: Basic Books.

CHAPTER 3

Phase Two
AUTONOMY

> The goal of Phase Two is to help children develop a sense of their unique, independent selves.

The goal of Phase Two is to help children develop a sense of their unique, independent selves. During Phase One, children learn to separate from parents because we provide them with a consistent teacher to whom they can attach and a classroom environment that is safe and secure. As this trust is established and the children feel safe and provided for within the group, they gain confidence in feeling accepted for who they are and start to express their own unique ideas and initiative. However, children still need support from teachers in bolstering a sense that it is OK to try new things. In this process of trying new things and sometimes failing, children may feel frustrated and angry. When children feel this way, they often act out these emotions and can provoke strong reactions in teachers who are responsible for helping them safely play and learn. This is a stormy time for children, who continue to need teachers to help them delay immediate gratification and live through the often-intense reactions that limits continue to evoke. In children who have more mature coping skills, these reactions are relatively short-lived, but the distress can be prolonged and painful for children who do not seem to have these skills, and it can almost seem contagious in the classroom. Teachers must often manage their own feelings when these emotional reactions seem out of control. Teachers who continue to do a daily check-in of children's feelings during the morning circle time often report that children are increasingly able to express their deeper emotions during Phase Two.

Developmental Focus: Independence Days

Throughout Phase Two and beyond, teachers and staff work together as providers of:

- Firm and gentle limits
- Clear expectations
- Optimal distance (not too close and not too far)
- Flexibility
- Balance between holding on and letting go
- Sense of humor

Once children have begun to master separation from their caregivers and feel secure in their attachments to teachers, they feel more comfortable exploring their environment and trying new things. When children are secure in their relationship with teachers, they are freer to develop peer relationships. At this point, they *know* that Mommy comes back. Much like toddlers who feel increasingly confident in testing boundaries and seeing what they can do for themselves, children in Phase Two feel safe that teachers will be able to give them the space to experiment but still set reasonable limits. This is not an easy process for teachers, as often children also feel more secure to act out in a safe environment. Children in this phase are figuring out who they are in the context of the group, and there is more awareness of other children. They are excited to talk about themselves; play out their own ideas; and explore their likes, dislikes, and preferences in relation to other children in the group. They also express more of their difficulties, and teachers often ask where their well-behaved classroom went!

WHAT YOU MIGHT WORRY ABOUT:

The children are feeling comfortable in the environment, so you might see more assertive behavior. It might be louder. Children might be sassier; you will see some defiance. This is all developmentally appropriate.

WEBSTER'S DICTIONARY DEFINES AUTONOMY AS HAVING THREE ELEMENTS:

Self-governance,
Self-Direction, and
Moral Independence

Can you think of a midyear example of this in your classroom?

Typical Child Behaviors: "I Can Do It Myself!"

- Developing individuality and autonomy
- Testing limits
- Experimentation, exploration, and messiness
- Developing confidence and competence
- Self-control with self-esteem
- Group formation: managing alliances, enemies, and rivalries ("us against them")
- Asserting individual preferences

The task for children during Phase Two is to feel confident and competent enough to experiment with being oppositional and to test out separateness from adults. In this process of telling teachers their own ideas, they continue to use teachers' limits to gain self-control without losing self-esteem. Sometimes, this can result in intense power struggles with teachers or competition with other children. Self-esteem is maintained when children are not given a message that they are "bad" or that they will receive harsh punishment for exploring these limits.

TEACHER'S RESPONSES: PATIENCE IS A VIRTUE
- Self-awareness
- Holding structure with appropriate flexibility
- Firm, gentle limits
- Clear expectations stated ahead of time
- Recognizing group contagion
- Balancing between holding on and letting go
- Balancing between closeness and distance
- Authority with empathy for the child's emotional experience
- Sense of humor

This can be a challenging time of year, but it is important for the child's development. It's hard to hold onto the idea that children's defying limits actually represents a deepening of your relationship. This is just a phase, and while it can't be skipped, it too will pass. Children test limits during this phase. If you are able to maintain the structure and routine of your classroom, in a calm way, children will start to internalize these limits and eventually will start to manage their own behavior. It's important to recognize that attaining a stance of patience will help you in navigating children's burgeoning sense of autonomy. At this point in the year, children know you well enough to know what pushes your buttons. Here is an example of how defying limits in Phase Two can be a sign of growing autonomy and assertiveness:

> *Alex and Sammy are building a massive structure in the block area. They have taken out nearly all of the blocks. Ms. Polly sings the warning song that it's five minutes until the cleanup time. Ms. Polly is known to like a clean classroom. The boys continue to play. To the outside observer they appear to ignore her warning. Five minutes pass and the lights flicker signaling time to clean up and everyone, except Alex and Sammy, sing the clean up song. Instead, Alex and Sammy sing loudly, "NO, NO, NO!" Ms. Polly starts to get annoyed and takes a deep breath as she approaches the boys. She says, "Boys, your structure is beautiful, how about I take a picture of it before you clean it up." Sammy falls to the ground and starts to cry. Alex goes over to Sammy and pats him on the shoulder saying, "She is going to take a picture!"*

WATCH AND WONDER: QUESTIONS TO ASK
- Why was it hard for Alex and Sammy to stop their play?
- What was Ms. Polly feeling?
- How did Ms. Polly manage her feelings and respond to Alex and Sammy?
- Why did Ms. Polly say she would take a picture of the block structure?

Once children have developed an attachment to their classroom teachers, they begin to feel comfortable pushing limits. Alex and Sammy ignored Ms. Polly's warning but her calm response and acknowledgement of their feelings helped this situation to stay under control. Teachers must develop ways to intervene early in helping to calm and contain children who are acting out, as often other children will start up, and the group can feel chaotic. Children will often have patterns of when they act out, and teachers can start to feel more proactive when they plan ahead for managing these reactions, instead of waiting until the situation feels out of control. Teachers can remind the children of the rules, routine, and where they should be, verbalizing expectations that the group can remain in control and can be safe even when one child is experiencing intense feelings and acting out. This anchors children when emotions threaten to make them and the teachers feel ungrounded. Children often get anxious when another child is out of control, and they might either imitate the behavior or show their own nervous feelings in other similarly disruptive ways. Also, children sometimes imitate or "try on" the behaviors of a child who frequently acts out. Teachers can simply remind the others that they have their own feelings and ideas and do not need to imitate others. Children typically cycle through these imitative behaviors quickly with teachers' help.

Teachers can use humor and connection with each other to avoid feeling personally attacked by children testing limits in intense and trying ways. Sometimes, children's struggles to assert themselves can be cute and funny. While we do not want to laugh directly at them, a chuckle inside and saving these stories to share with colleagues can help you maintain perspective. Laughing with them can help you appreciate this phase and can endear you to children's frustrations and attempts to work through them. You must not lose sight of the fact that children who feel safe testing limits with you are actually demonstrating that your relationships are strong and that they trust you to respond in a way that is safe for them, both physically and emotionally.

Teachers can often feel overwhelmed and exhausted during this phase, and it is important that you have healthy outlets for relieving stress. Work with children naturally pulls on your emotions as a human being. Optimally, your administration and fellow teachers foster an environment where you can talk about this and gain support to not feel alone in the day-to-day struggles during Phase Two. Perhaps others have found ways of responding to behaviors, and their creative suggestions can help you feel like you have more strategies in your toolbox for managing these intense moments.

ROUTINES: COMMUNITY ACTION!
- Large group activities
- Greater focus on sharing and waiting

Phase Two AUTONOMY

- Jobs and increased responsibility
- Subgrouping

From Phase One with its focus on consistent and predictable routines, a safe environment, and teacher support, children have a basic sense of belonging in the classroom community. Phase Two offers the chance for children to explore roles and express more individuality within this community. Teachers need to continue consistent and predictable routines. When changes are made, teachers should continue to tell children in advance why things are changing and how the group will respond to the changes. Morning check-ins offer children opportunities to express a wide range of feelings (Kriete 2002). Now that children are familiar with the basic structure and routine of the day, they are ready to take added responsibility in the classroom. Children like to have regularly rotating jobs to feel a part of the group. A child develops a sense of pride and ownership in mastering simple tasks and feels important in making a contribution for the common good of the classroom. In addition to these jobs, teachers can also enlist help by giving simple tasks during transitions, such as asking a child who looks distracted to put something in a specific bin. Children are more aware and interested in their peers and are ready for more large-group activities during Phase Two. Children are eager to play games such as duck-duck-goose that encourage sitting and waiting and sequencing action. In Phase Two, as in all the phases, teachers should gauge when children are ready for theses expanded activities. If the group starts to become agitated, trying something again when the group is able to do it in a calm way is OK.

ENVIRONMENT: MORE IS GOOD

- Provide emotional and physical space for moving away from teachers
- Give more choices
- Provide product-oriented activities and skill-building opportunities
- Give firm but flexible structure

During Phase Two, teachers encourage children to be more active in shaping the environment. Teachers allow more space for children to move away from them to explore their own unique interests. This does not mean creating a gym in the classroom; it does mean assessing whether children's interests can shape the environment in meaningful ways, such as by adding play areas or art stations so that children have expanded choices. Since some group games that include more body movements are introduced in this phase, teachers might need to create a larger space for children to move around. Choices expand into creative pursuits that are more product-driven rather than process-focused. In Phase One, we focused on simple activities where children explored materials and made things that were not permanent. The focus was on feeling calm and using things that grounded them in the moment. In Phase Two, children are better able to plan to make projects with an end result in mind. They can take pride in bringing these projects home to parents or hanging them on the classroom walls. Teachers should create areas to store creative projects and to display finished products with pride. Remember children will still need clear limits during this phase.

CURRICULUM PRESENTATION: EXERCISE YOUR RIGHT TO CHOOSE!

- Provide more complicated projects
- Give more choices for open-ended projects
- Allow for activities that promote experimentation and messiness
- Plan group activities that require more turn-taking and waiting

In Phase Two, teachers start to encourage and support increased autonomy. By autonomy, we mean, the ability to manage oneself emotionally, cooperate, and be able to make good choices. This is based on the balance between one's own needs and ideas and the wish to be part of a group. Successful independent actions can become the building blocks of autonomy. Phase Two can be a stormy phase where teachers encounter children's need to express their individuality and sometimes challenge teachers' ideas. Teachers who weather this storm with grace and a sense of humor can provide activities that direct some of this energy into games and projects that allow children more control.

Art projects and larger constructions that extend over multiple days allow for children to expand their creative horizons. In Phase Two, children who can continue projects over multiple days learn about the passage of time and work on delaying gratification. When they save their projects for the next day, children demonstrate a strong sense of security that everything will still be there when they return to the classroom. This is a time when teachers should promote children's interests as to what toys and art materials are in the classroom. As children develop more autonomy, they will test more limits. This may come as a surprise, but maintain your cool and set firm and clear limits.

Phase Two Activities

At this time of year, children are beginning to assert their autonomy through experimentation and individual preferences. Providing a wide range of materials and projects where they can focus and further develop their emerging skills is key during Phase Two.

Example sensory activities:
- Play dough (extruders—plastic garlic press, making own play dough as a group)
- Water (sometimes group water table)

- Sand table (or bins)
- Bins with bubble wrap
- Mystery box

Example art activities:
- Watercolors (more elaborate than first phase—children paint their own pictures)
- Sponge painting, printing
- Easel painting (children's requests, "favorites," or your own ideas)
- Cut-and-paste projects (snowmen, teddy bears, more complex patterns)
- Glue projects (popsicle stick houses, collages)
- Making necklaces
- Paper strip constructions

Example academic and constructive exploration activities:
- Cooking (more complex recipes, some requiring one day to complete—e.g., bread)
- Hammer and nail sets (with or without patterns, can be expanded into making a project)
- Blocks (large and unit), trains, and so on.
- Writing and drawing books (following teacher's model, teacher writes what child dictates)
- Games and dramatic play
- Doll corner, house play
- Board games (with teacher direction, as a group)
- Duck-duck-goose
- Bean bags (tossing, passing, putting on body parts)
- Act out simple stories or tales
- Red light, green light

Phase Two Books

During Phase Two, books can be longer and more complicated. They deal with phase-specific issues such as aggression, anger, autonomy, and curiosity. Examples include the following:

- Rainey Bennett, *The Secret Hiding Place*
- John Burningham, *Mr. Gumpy's Outing*

- Paul Caldone, *The Little Red Hen*
- Eric Carle, *From Head to Toe*
- Mem Fox, *Harriet, You'll Drive Me Wild!*
- John E. Johnson, *I Like a Whole One*
- Ruth Krauss, *The Carrot Seed*
- Leo Lionni, *It's Mine*
- Arnold Lobel, *Small Pig*
- Bill Martin and John Archambault, *Chicka, Chicka, Boom, Boom*
- Arlene Mosel, *Tikki Tikki Tembo*
- Dr. Seuss, *Green Eggs and Ham*
- J. Slepian and A. Seidler, *The Hungry Thing*
- E. Slobodkina, *Caps for Sale*
- Janice Udry, *Let's Be Enemies*
- Judith Viorst, *I'll Fix Anthony!*
- Judith Viorst, *The Goodbye Book*
- Barbara Williams, *Gary and the Very Terrible Monster*
- Audrey Wood, *King Bidgood's in the Bathtub*
- Gene Zion, *Harry the Dirty Dog*
- Charlotte Zolotow, *The Hating Book*

Phase Two Songs

Phase Two songs focus on giving children more choices and challenges. Turn-taking songs and songs with instruments can be added here. Typical songs may focus on autonomy, using humor to say "no," and creative expression of different feelings and moods. Counting-off rhymes and other songs that focus on "knowing what is coming next" are also included. Examples include the following:

- "Five Little Monkeys"
- "Punchinello/Little Clown"
- "Hokey-Pokey"
- "I've Been Working on the Railroad"
- "B-I-N-G-O"

Phase Two Conclusion

Phase Two expands on the framework established in Phase One: a secure attachment to the teacher allows for independence. Children now feel secure in their environment and are open to the complex learning that is the hallmark of Phase Two. The timing of this Phase varies, depending on a child's length in the program and age. Children who are returning to your classroom may enter Phase Two more quickly than a child who is newer to your program or younger in age or developmental level. Think of Phase One as getting-to-know-you time and Phase Two as a time to move toward independence. This helps you assess where individual children and the group as a whole are during this middle phase of the year. Teachers need to be able to balance holding and letting go. Teachers represent a "secure base" from which children explore their environment (Bowlby 1988). In this process, teachers provide games, songs, and activities that promote experimentation with independence and autonomy. Teachers are often tested in this phase, and we recommend that you pay attention to your own emotions and self-care during this time, as children provoke strong reactions. Weathering this phase helps children experience your limits from the outside and then gradually internalize them and experience increasing self-control. If done well, the limit-testing during Phase Two leads to a stronger attachment between children and teachers. Teachers can take pride in each child's development of greater self-control, a stronger sense of self, and a greater sense of right and wrong. These new and expanded skills contribute to the consolidation of the classroom during Phase Three.

References

Bowlby, John. 1988. *A Secure Base: Parent-Child Attachment and Healthy Human Development.* London: Basic Books.

Kriete, Roxann. 2002. *The Morning Meeting Book.* Turner Falls: Northeast Foundation for Children, Inc.

CHAPTER 4

Phase Three
INITIATIVE & INDEPENDENCE

> **The goal of Phase Three is to help children consolidate and integrate what they have learned during the year and say good-bye.**

The goal of Phase Three is to help children consolidate and integrate what they have learned during the year and say good-bye. The dreary days of winter pass, and so, too, do the storms of Phase Two. By spring, the children in your program have probably tested every limit in the classroom and have tried your last nerves. You and they have survived all this turmoil and are looking forward to sunnier days. Phase Three is a time of blossoming of children's autonomy, initiative, independence, and capacity to cope with loss and change without falling apart. Phase Three is the final third of your program year, usually in the late spring and summer.

During Phase Three we have the themes of autonomy and integrating skills and relationship capacities that are the foundation for classroom learning. Children are able to attend to more complex projects, tasks, and ideas and can make more meaningful contributions to discussions. They have integrated a sense of their own place in the community of the classroom. Hopefully, you as the teacher can stand back with your co-teachers and start to enjoy the unique individuals that the children are. They will give you pleasure that you never imagined possible earlier in the year.

Good-byes are the ultimate transitions. The loss of the classroom where children have felt comfortable and loved will be big in their young lives.

Even if they express a lot of excitement about going on to another classroom or a "big school," children may have a nervous feeling too. Preparing them and their parents for this transition is important, as the parents will be with their children through many transitions and can use this experience to help children with transitions throughout their lives.

At this phase children consolidate information and are able to take in new information and use it to expand on their play themes. They look toward adults for validation of their wonderful ideas and take pleasure in their mastery.

WEBSTER'S DICTIONARY DEFINES INITIATIVE AS

energy or aptitude displayed in initiation of action.

Can you think of an end-of-the-year example of this in your classroom?

Four little girls in your class sing all the time. One day they ask you, "What's a concert?" You reply, "Well, a person or people who get together to sing songs for an audience." "Oh, like we were in the audience when we saw that play in winter." "Yes," you reply. Whispering ensues, then, "Can we do a concert for you and the other kids?" You beam, "What a great idea! How about at outside time?" That day they take hairbrushes from their cubbies and use them as microphones. They sway together for an appreciative audience of their peers, who clap to the sounds of the latest pop songs.

Developmental Focus: Initiative and Independence

Throughout Phase Three teachers and staff facilitate and appreciate children's development of the following:

- Initiative and independence
- Internalization of rules
- The emergence of conscience (knowing right and wrong)
- Gender identity
- The ability to say good-bye

In Phases One and Two, we focused more on what the teachers provide. You will notice the bullet points above are child-focused. By Phase Three, most children have internalized the rules of the classroom. They do not need the teachers to remind them of the rules; they know them, which is a big step in developing initiative. When children have initiative, they take the lead and complete tasks without being asked. This is an important step in working toward school readiness, as teachers will not always be by the children's sides to guide them throughout the school day.

Children are more emotionally free at this time of the year because they have successfully gone through the first two phases. They have more emotional and psychological capacity to come up with their own ideas for activities and to explore their blossoming interests. This means they can be more self-directing.

By Phase Three, children will have developed self-awareness and the awareness of others' feelings and thoughts. With this ability to care about each other, children know when they are acting in a kind manner, and this means they have achieved greater moral independence and the developmental of inner controls. This is the burgeoning development of the ability to know right from wrong. Phase Three is also a time when children demonstrate caring and a deep understanding of each other's likes, dislikes, strengths, and weaknesses.

At this time of year, children are starting to notice gender differences and are identifying themselves as boys or girls. You will hear in your classroom phrases such as, "Only boys on the rug today, playing with the big blocks. No girls allowed!"

WHAT YOU MIGHT WORRY ABOUT:

Some teachers worry that talking about upcoming good-byes will worry children or make it harder for them to feel excited about moving on to a new school in the future. Children who are excited are also usually nervous about saying good-bye to you and going to a new school. You might also worry about expressing your own feelings about the good-bye to children, but we know that children can pick up on our feelings whether we put words to them or not. Talking about the mixed feelings stirred up by good-byes and feelings about loss, endings, and future unknowns helps the classroom come together and celebrate successes.

TYPICAL BEHAVIORS: "LOOK WHAT I CAN DO!"
- Developing new skills and competencies
- Identifying with the group
- Taking initiative in doing "jobs" in the classroom
- Anxiety about endings

During Phase Three, most children express their own ideas and assess their own competence more accurately than earlier in the year. Whereas in the earlier phases, some children boasted about skills they wished they had, such as running faster than everyone else, during Phase Three children are eager to share a more realistic picture of what they can do and be praised for and accepted for this. Phase Three involves more group consensus, and children can work with others in the classroom to generate ideas, request activities, help each other accomplish goals and tasks, and share materials. Children crave opportunities for independence and often take pride in being given added responsibilities for classroom jobs.

Phase Three INITIATIVE & INDEPENDENCE

Children may have preferences for their friends in the classroom and with whom they like to play at certain times of the day. Classmates are an important source of feedback and emotional reciprocity during this phase. Emotional reciprocity involves the give-and-take of caring for others. Children will complement each other on a job well done or tell the teacher when their friend gets hurt on the playground. This happens when teachers provide the model for emotional openness and caregiving that children need in order to be able to give to each other at this stage in the year. All that work you did during Phase One to ensure the children that you have enough attention and caring to meet all their needs pays off when you see them even use the same words of comfort you once gave them when caring for one another. You as a teacher can observe this and praise them for learning how to be so good to one another!

In Phase Three, teachers and staff help children and parents:

- Anticipate what will come next for the child
- Assess where the child is at developmentally and in learning activities
- Get help for children who continue to struggle
- Recognize and process feelings around good-byes
- Feel a sense of accomplishment of all the child has done over the year
- Get the resources to make a smooth transition to kindergarten, if applicable
- Manage regression around the good-bye

The transition to kindergarten means many changes for parents as well as children. Parents' routines change when getting a child to a new school, and there are many new relationships in the new setting that parents also have to master before feeling comfortable with sending their child to a new school. First-time parents may not feel secure that they know what to expect when moving to a bigger school system and getting all the needed documents to the new school. Some parents have to say good-bye to other parents whom they have come to know around drop-off and pick-up time.

Many children experience some end-of-the-year regression around major transitions and good-byes (even if it is just a good-bye for one month and they will return the next year). Regression in preschoolers is linked to insecurities children have about their attachment to important caregivers in their lives and often involves acting, thinking, and feeling like a child who is developmentally younger (Davies 1999). Examples include having wetting accidents when a new baby is born in the family or the night before the last day of school. It makes sense that this would happen when children are facing a good-bye to a teacher they have depended upon and loved over the course of a program year. It's almost like the children are reminding you that there is a younger part of them that doesn't feel quite grown-up enough to take of themselves and that is asking you to be aware of that need even if they have developed a lot of other capacities over the year. These regressions can really confuse and worry parents who thought their children had grown out of certain behaviors. The parents often need your help to know that these are temporary regressions and that children do not lose what they have gained.

TEACHERS RESPONSES: "YES, YOU CAN!"
- Self-awareness
- Encouraging group interaction
- Facilitating group problem solving
- Verbalizing and accepting children's feelings around the good-bye

Teachers often can relax a little during Phase Three and can take a step back to watch and enjoy children's ability to manage themselves in the now-familiar classroom. Mastery is the aim during Phase Three, and teachers continue to provide opportunities for children to practice what they know and expand their interests and talents by providing new challenges.

Children love when teachers can follow their lead at this stage because children who have been guided through Phases One and Two are now feeling safe to explore with one another. If they feel secure, children will generate exciting ideas for activities, games, and conversations. When we say teachers can relax, we mean that teachers can enjoy letting children lead, while recognizing that the children still need guidance along the way.

Watch and Wonder: Questions to Ask

When children are getting ready to transition out of your classroom, here are some questions to consider.

- What are the child's strengths and challenges?
- Is the child progressing at a similar rate to others in the classroom, or is there an issue that might need to be explored that is holding this particular child back?
- Is the parent involved and active in planning for the child's next step?
- Can the child tell you what will be happening the next school year (e.g., does the child know the school's name and the teacher's name; can the child tell you about the school)?
- Does the parent need resources or guidance?
- Does the child need an individualized education plan or outside therapy to help to transition to school or make more progress in your program next year?

Teachers need to be the leaders in talking about transitions to new schools and the good-byes with children and their parents. Preschoolers are at an age where they are still learning how to have mixed feelings. Mixed feelings—such as being sad to leave trusted teachers but excited to go to the big school with the awesome playground—are very common in good-byes. Activities, art projects, circle time discussions, books, and songs are opportunities to explore the mixed feelings children and teachers often have about the latter part of the year.
You can talk about how it's confusing to have more than one feeling at a time. Children will find ways of trying to anticipate what the next step will be, such as telling stories to each other about how big brothers or sisters went to school on the bus or had such-and-such teacher. As a teacher, you can balance the urge to explore what comes next with talk about what children have learned

over the year. You can give children assurance that they will get to know their new teachers and classmates just as they did in your classroom. Children love that caring adults can remember what they were like at the beginning of the year and how much they've grown. Photos of the beginning can be helpful in reminding yourself of how a child has grown and how their interests and skills have evolved over the course of the year. Parents welcome this reflection, too, as they wonder how their children will manage the next phase.

Knowing What to Expect Makes Children Feel Safe

You might be glad a child who has presented challenges over the year will be moving on, or you might be very sad a child who you feel particularly attached to is leaving. Maybe you saw big strides in a child who has developmental challenges, and you worry about him or her being labeled in the new school. You will have feelings about the ending, just as the children do. You can talk about the ending with your co-staff or supervisor. To express some of the thoughts and feelings about the year, some staff members like to write good-bye letters that include photos. Making a good-bye song CD can help everyone reflect and share a collective good-bye. We recommend encouraging children to express their feelings through hugs and tears and to recognize both the positive and the negative feelings of good-byes.

ROUTINES: EXPANDING THE CHILDREN'S WORLD
- More flexibility
- Changes in schedule to accommodate larger explorations and projects
- Field trips
- Practicing separation within school

During Phase Three, children have reached a developmental level where they have the capacity to come in with ideas about play themes, listen to others' ideas, and negotiate throughout the day. Because of the children's developmental capacities, transitions flow with ease, creating more time for expanded activities. This time allows children to build on each other's ideas.

Field trips provide children with the opportunity to flex their internalized self-control and sense of identity. Because of these skills, they are well able to enjoy what the field trip has to offer, and they can enjoy being out in the world.

Phase Three: INITIATIVE & INDEPENDENCE

In addition, giving children the opportunity to move out of the classroom to the larger school helps them to practice independence and responsibility, which is a precursor to transitioning to a new classroom or kindergarten.

ENVIRONMENT: EXPANDING THEIR HORIZONS
- Allow children to reconstruct or rearrange space
- Expand classroom space (such as to hallways and other parts of building)

This is the time of year where the classroom can seem like the set of an ever-changing play. For example, the dramatic play area might be reconstructed into a doctor's office, a restaurant, or a beauty shop. Children will often come up with ideas for making murals and constructions that include other significant parts of their world. This can include constructing mailboxes in front of the secretary's door or constructing an Internet café.

CURRICULUM PRESENTATION: CHILDREN TAKE CHARGE
- Include group creative experiences/plays
- Group art projects/murals
- Include child-initiated curricular ideas
- Creating books, reviewing the year, anticipating the future

The hallmark of the Phase Three curriculum is group process, as the children take ownership of what happens in the classroom. They present ideas and negotiate with peers and teachers to propel the action in the classroom. Because children are so internally calm and externally focused, their imaginations blossom. This is evidenced in the classroom by children making up plays, building edifices and objects, and writing books that review their year. As a result, the Phase Three classroom is abuzz with activity. Because children are so comfortable within themselves and the classroom, they are able to anticipate the future, which may include transitioning to a new classroom or kindergarten.

Phase Three Activities

Activity time in Phase Three is often a time of high-level functioning. At this point in the year, children have good ideas, want to take initiative, and are competent in carrying out their plans. A classroom environment supportive of this growth and development allows children to receive recognition for their accomplishments and feel good about their achievements.

Example sensory activities:
- Water table
- Sand table
- Planting
- Cooking, with children involved in all the steps

Example art activities:
- Group murals/map
- Woodworking
- Cardboard box constructions
- Large paper fish mobiles

Example academic and constructive explorations
- Doll corner
- Blocks, Lincoln Logs, and trains
- Reading and math groups
- Books (own ideas)
- Trips away from the classroom (park, store, etc.)
- Board games
- Planting
- Body tracing
- Legos
- Creating and acting out own stories

Phase Three Books

Phase Three books can be longer and chosen to promote group discussion and interaction. The books include fairy tales and other stories about which the children can ask open-ended questions. Children are interested in the content of the stories in this phase and enjoy discussing them and making connections with real experiences. Books may deal with phase-appropriate themes, such as rivalry, friendship, trying new things, and growing up/saying good-bye. In addition to the examples below, books from Phase One should be included as a way of reviewing the year and addressing children's separation needs.

- Lorraine Aseltine, *First Grade Can Wait*
- Virginia Lee Burton, *The Little House*
- Virginia Lee Burton, *Mike Mulligan and His Steam Shovel*
- Eric Carle, *A House for a Hermit Crab*
- Lauren Child, *I Am Too Absolutely Small for School*
- Tomie DePaola, *Strega Nona*
- P. Galdone, *The Three Billy Goats Gruff*
- *Goldilocks and the Three Bears*
- Juanita Havill, *Jamaica's Find*
- Russell Hoban, *Frances* (series)
- Ezra Jack Keats, –*Peter's Chair*
- Munro Leaf, *The Story of Ferdinand*
- Leo Lionni, *Swimmy*
- Leo Lionni, *Tillie and the Wall*
- Arnold Lobel, *Frog and Toad* (series)
- Robert McCloskey, *Make Way for Ducklings*
- Watty Piper, *The Little Engine that Could*
- Dr. Seuss, *The Cat in the Hat*
- Marjorie Sharmat, *I Don't Care*
- Norma Simon, *Nobody's Perfect, Not Even My Mother*
- William Steig, *Boris & Amos*
- William Steig, *Sylvester and the Magic Pebble*
- Carla Stevens, *Hooray for Pig*
- Janice Udry, *What Mary Jo Shared*
- Judith Viorst, *The Good-bye Book*

Phase Three Songs

Children are given more freedom during Phase Three music time. Songs and games can be used that encourage expression of feelings and require cooperation. This is a time for experimentation, in terms of both movement activities and creating new verses for songs. Children will enjoy working with a variety of instruments. This is a good time to give children the opportunity to choose songs and perhaps lead the group. Toward the end of the school year, it will become important to revisit songs from Phase One as separation issues, once again, become more pronounced. Examples include the following:

- "Zudio"
- "John Brown's Baby"
- "Hide the Tamborine"
- "Jim Along Josie" (complicated version with partners)
- "Paw-Paw Patch"
- Old songs with new twist, such as having parades, adding instruments, marching, etc.
- "Row Your Boat" (with partners)
- "Did You Feed My Cow?"
- "London Bridge Is Falling Down"
- "Rest Time" (teacher comfort/child comfort)
- "Hush Little Baby"
- Pachelbel's "Canon in D"
- "Once I Had a Little Dog"
- "Edelweiss"
- Folk songs, such as those on *Peter, Paul and Mommy*
- Ella Jenkins, "Rhythm of Childhood"
- Pete Seeger songs
- "Yonder She Comes"

Phase Three Conclusion

Phase Three expands on the framework established in Phase One and Phase Two. Children have gone from separation and attachment to an ability to explore various roles and express more individuality in the classroom community. In Phase Three children are able to consolidate all the learning they have engaged in throughout the year. The hallmark of Phase Three is an integration of past experiences which children can utilize to come up with original ideas and activities. At this time of year, walking into a classroom the visitor should be thrust into an atmosphere of energized activity and joy. Children are also saying good-bye. They are now able to manage their feelings in a direct and articulate way. Teachers who have successfully addressed the social and emotional needs of children throughout the year, will feel a sense of accomplishment as Phase Three ends.

References

Davies, Douglas. 1999. *Child Development: A Practitioner's Guide*. New York: Guilford Press.

CHAPTER 5

Incorporating Morning Check-In Concepts Into Your Classroom

> *The Relationship-Based Phase Model* came out of the work we do as mental health consultants to preschools in Chicago (Kriete 1999).

The genesis of the use of some of the concepts of "morning check-in" in conjunction with *Connections: The Relationship-Based Phase Model* came out of the work we do as mental health consultants to preschools in Chicago (Kriete 1999). We read Kriete's *The Morning Meeting Book*, which is designed for children in kindergarten through grade 8. We were so impressed with it that we have adapted some ideas and concepts of Morning Meeting to help teachers become more aware of the complicated feelings that children can bring into their school setting.

As mental health consultants, we are charged with observing children individually, should parents, site directors and teachers have concerns regarding a child's development or behavior in the classroom.

One school year, lead teacher Ms. Adelina and long-time mental health consultant Joanne had a very interesting conversation. It was the beginning of the school year, and Ms. Adelina stated somewhat worriedly, "Joanne, I'm thinking about referring about six children to you for individual observations. I've been wondering how it is that so many kids could be in such distress and displaying their unhappiness so vividly in the classroom each day." They explored further just what was transpiring with each child and came up with the following list:

- Loud responses from many children at each transition
- Children hitting each other seemingly without provocation
- Children grabbing toys from each other without even an attempt at using language to secure what they wanted.

Joanne, Ms. Adelina and Ms Hanka met regularly with the site director. This was important so the director could support the teacher's work during the course of the week and address issues in reflective supervision. Ms. Adelina had tried many of the suggestions that Joanne had offered over the years and had a solid understanding of the Phase Model. Joanne said that she had heard about an idea that went beyond what Ms. Adelina had already tried to address more global kinds of classroom distress. They decide to investigate and try out some activities in the morningcheck-in model in her classroom. Ms. Adelina was intrigued. We opened up this opportunity to the other teachers at the site, and Ms. Hanka wanted to be a part of our investigation, too.

Here are the basic steps to incorporate concepts of morning check-in in your classroom:

Step One: Make a feelings chart.
- Make a feelings chart with faces corresponding to emotions.
- Attach Velcro strips next to the faces.
- Laminate children's names (or photos) for use in the following activity.

Step Two: Use yourself as an example.
- During the initial circle time, begin first with yourself; talk about how your morning has gone and attach an emotion to your experiences.
- Put your name on the chart under the emotion face that corresponds best to your feelings that morning.

Step Three: Go around the circle.
- Encourage the children to talk about their morning and put their name under the appropriate emotion on the chart.
- Practice validating and accepting the emotion the child expresses without trying to fix or question.

Ms. Adelina and Ms. Hanka with the assistance of Joanne, mental health consultant, began using morning check-in. Ms. Adelina opened morning meeting with, "Oh, I was so frustrated this morning because I had a hard time starting my car," attaching her name to the picture of frustration, then adding, "but I'm so happy to be with you all this morning." The children caught on to this format and added their own experiences as they were called on in the group.

After the teachers did this every morning for two weeks, they sat down with Joanne, the site director, and their colleagues to process their experience experimenting with morning check-in. The discussion focused on the teachers' feelings when children shared difficult material during the meeting. Ms. Adelina and Ms. Hanka recognized that often children shared family feelings that they did not necessarily understand but felt very intensely and often acted out in the classroom. The teachers were amazed at how children with few language skills were able to express a lot more using the pictures and feelings chart. Ms. Adelina and Ms. Hanka also reflected on how they felt that they were more responsible for children's feelings because they knew more about the children's lives. The children had started to trust in the teachers' ability to listen more deeply to their feelings and experiences. Ms. Adelina shared, "It's a big load. We're left with the families' feelings. Even as self-aware adults, we can get edgy, mean, or absent-minded when we have a lot on our minds. But kids don't yet have the capacity to understand why they're 'acting out;' they just do it because they've heard or witnessed or been a part of events that they don't understand and that morning check-in can give them a forum for talking about and sharing." The group agreed that this activity speaks to the feelings and worries that may be underneath children's stories and can help them work through the anxiety that's being expressed. The teachers responded to the children by saying simple things such as "I know it's scary when mommies and daddies fight," and "It's safe here and we are here to listen. We don't fight here—we talk when we disagree." They shared that reflecting on and speaking to the children's underlying emotions really helped the children.

Because the teachers felt support from the mental health consultant and the site director, they were willing to engage in this very different use of themselves. The support came in the form of encouragement, acceptance and validation of the teacher's feelings, and safety.

Everyone agreed that it helped to remember that their job is to hear and validate feelings and not to fix the situation. They agreed that this is the key to helping to restrict the anxiety that can become so contagious in a classroom. The group also touched upon how preschoolers often copy one another, with one child saying something and then the others saying the same thing. The teachers agreed that the children were conveying something and eliciting attention, and that a teacher's nonjudgmental responses start to get at the message communicated underneath what a child is repeating. Children want attention, to talk, and to be heard. Sometimes, this means borrowing a story or words from another, but they are practicing how to tell their story in the morning check-in flow nonetheless. One teacher shared, "They want attention…and we know that all kids want attention. It doesn't matter what kind—negative or positive—and we can respond within the context of a relationship. When a child is new to the classroom they need to (1) understand what's transpiring in the environment, (2) fit in, and (3) get the 'protocol.' This will sometimes bring about the 'copying.'" This teacher also noted that language is all around us. Even if a child who was called upon wasn't focused in on the morning check-in, that child might have heard or remembered what some other child said, leading him or her to repeat it. Did you ever walk down the street chatting with a friend and, as another duo passes you by, you say some words from the passing conversation instead of what you were intending to say? Words are intended to connect us, and children experience this without as many filters, at times.

The following vignette illustrates how morning check-in can help a preschooler restrain anxiety and feel ready for learning for the rest of the day:

> *Three-and-a-half-year-old Joseph, who comes to Head Start each day with lots energy and lots of ideas, was unable to play cooperatively in any area of the classroom. When he initiates a play theme in a particular area of the room, it must be facilitated by an adult. With the adult narrating and helping to facilitate negotiations between children with whom he is engaging, he does OK. When the*

> *adult leaves the area, within a short period of time he snatches toys, begins to loudly try to control the play, [and] is unable to take turns, let alone listen to another's idea. Pretty quickly others are calling for help. There's often a smile on his face upon the teacher's return. Even if she admonishes him, helps him to share, to apologize, or [to] look at his playmates' perspective, he is often happy.*
>
> *As a result of morning check-in, Joseph was able to express his feelings and then go on about the business of play. We could say in essence that he felt trust that his teachers could help him manage his feelings.,"*

Play can flow from the morning check-in, as children take up themes that they wish to work through. For example, a child who shared a story about a police arrest might play with a group of children about this arrest following the morning check-in, and teachers can key into the connections and tie the talk about it with the subsequent play on the same theme. Play becomes richer when teachers understand why children are interested in the themes that they play. Teachers also recognize through using morning check-in that children have lighter emotional loads when playing these themes, as they have a chance to process their emotions around experiences that provoke strong feelings.

What Children Learn through Participating in Morning Check-In Activities

Neuroscience research on brain development has shown that preschoolers' brains are malleable and that the prefrontal cortex of the brain, which houses the skills required for executive functioning can change in the context of a healthy early attachment. The National Center for Learning Disabilities defines executive functioning as a set of mental processes that helps connect past experiences with present action. In his book *How Children Succeed*, Paul Tough says, "The reason that researchers who care about the gap between rich and poor are so excited about executive functions is that these skills are not only highly predictive of success; they are also quite malleable, much more so than other cognitive skills...So if we can improve a child's environment in the specific ways that lead to better executive functioning, we can increase his prospects for success in a particularly efficient way." (Tough 2012) morning check-in promotes:

- Paying attention and focusing
- Practicing self-control
- Empathy
- Showing respect for themselves and others

How Morning Check-In Influences Academic and Executive Functioning Skills

For over fifty-five years, we here at the Virginia Frank Child Development Center have been intimately involved with early childhood professionals who, because of their training, often ask us, "What is this teaching the children?" The authors of *The Morning Meeting Book* have compiled the following wonderful list of teachable moments embedded in their Morning Meeting activity (Kreite 1999) and our morning check-in. Greeting—When children are greeting each other, they are learning to:

- Acknowledge others' presence as well as themselves
- Recognize names of classmates
- Be courteous, considerate, and caring
- Become comfortable in social situations
- Gain a sense of community and a feeling of belonging
- Gain self-esteem
- Speak clearly in an audible voice
- Make eye contact
- Wait their turn
- Pay attention and focus on the speaker
- Welcome classmates to the group
- Help classmates feel valued, liked, and wanted
- Practice self-control
- Understand spoken information
- Develop new and different ways to greet each other
- Show respect for themselves and others
- Develop sequencing skills

Sharing—When children are sharing, they are learning to:

- Develop communication skills in expressive and receptive language
- Develop leadership skills
- Organize ideas

- Respect the opinions, experiences, and cultures of others
- Be comfortable as the center of attention
- Distinguish between reality and fantasy
- Take turns
- Build self-esteem
- Develop empathy and compassion

Group Activity—When children participate in a group activity, they are learning to:

- Empathize
- Improve gross motor skills
- Increase muscle control, eye-hand coordination, and balance
- Build self-confidence
- Use language creatively
- Play and follow simple rules
- Identify patterns and sequences
- Participate in various games and activities both new and familiar
- Interact easily with classmates
- Participate in the group life of the classroom
- Participate in cooperative learning
- See the fun in learning and have a good time
- Support each other

We encourage teachers to think about how natural experiences, such as having these conversations with children during a morning check-in activity, promote fundamental learning experiences. Feeling validated in this way can create a feeling of well-being that allows children to be available for other cognitive pursuits throughout the day (Greenspan 2009). In this world of communication and connectivity, it is essential for children to be flexible and able to respond spontaneously, and this type of group provides them with a safe, easy way to practice expressing feelings, ideas, and stories about their lives. In classrooms using morning check-in, teachers often report that children are eager to have this time to talk and share with their teachers and each other. When Ms. Hanka from our example above polled her preschoolers on whether they wanted morning check-in or reviewing the monthly calendar, the children overwhelmingly chose morning check-in, highlighting its importance in the children's day.

References

Greenspan, S. 2009. *Building Healthy Minds: The Six Experiences That Create Intelligence and Emotional Growth in Babies and Young Children.* Boston: Da Capo Press.

Kriete, R. 1999. *The Morning Meeting Book.* Turner Falls, MA: Northeast Foundation for Children Inc.

The National Center for Learning Disabilities. 2013. Accessed December 26. http://www.ncld.org/.

Tough, P. 2012. *How Children Succeed.* New York: Houghton Mifflin Harcourt.

CHAPTER 6
Focus On Teachers

KEY POINTS FOR THIS CHAPTER
- This is hard work

- Self-awareness
- This work might make you angry
- Transference
- Reflective supervision
- Understanding trauma
- Cultural norms

- Staff processes and team building
- Administrative staff support

Self-Awareness

We who work with young children do so for a variety of reasons, and the reasons may change over time. Children bring an enormous amount of wonder and energy into a room. This can sometimes feel great and sometimes drain our energies and leave us feeling depleted. There are many factors that we can explore to understand our own feelings and motivations in this important and life-changing work. Let's take a look at some of the feelings and reactions that are normal for teachers throughout their careers and discover how you can feel more secure that your feelings and reactions are manageable and will actually empower you to do your job even better.

Our Behavior Has Meaning, Too

Recall that in Chapter 1, we discussed how all behavior has meaning for children. The same is true for adults, although we are more socialized and have more capacity for maintaining our cool even when we are feeling strong emotions. And *feel* we do! You might be surprised how you and other teachers differ about which children are your favorites or which children frustrate you. What we like and encourage in children is at the heart of who we are; it develops from how we were raised, what was encouraged in us by our parents and community, our basic temperaments, who children might remind us of in our own lives, how we manage and cope with stress, how much energy we have on a given day, what our health status is, how we get along and work with our co-teachers, how competent we feel, how our supervisors support or critique us, and more. The more awareness we have of why we feel the ways that we do, day-to-day and over the course of a school year, the more we can create a nurturing classroom where all children and staff can feel accepted and grow.

Developing self-awareness is a process of uncovering the root of our inner feelings toward the people we work with and the children we serve. Have you noticed that even children you find challenging in the beginning of the school term become likeable over the year if you feel like you can get in there, understand them, and help them learn? Or how an irritating coworker might become a friend after you have a deeper conversation and learn that she's had a recent tragedy in her life? When we understand ourselves, we can feel more in control of our emotions and can enjoy the experience of teaching young children. If we understand what is at the root of a feeling, we can start to recognize how our own behaviors stem from our feelings. Are there times when you get stuck and wish you could have a different response to a coworker or a child? Can you think of how you feel right before you want to snap or cry? What made you feel that way? Does it touch into something that happened earlier in your life, or some basic insecurity that you have about yourself? How is your reaction protecting you? How does it impact those around you? Let's think through some common emotions and possible triggers that touch into these.

"That Makes Me So Mad!"

Anger is considered by many mental health professionals to be a secondary emotion. In simple language, this means that there is usually some more primary (basic) fear or emotion that is underneath anger. Anger is useful because when a person feels threatened by either a situation or an emotion that feels too intense, it helps us act to protect ourselves. Think of anger as being an important part of our protective fight-or-flight response to danger. What does this have to do with working with young children, who we generally feel confident are not going to harm us? Because young children are not able to manage their own bodies in space and their own emotions very well, they need our protection. When we see them about to get hurt or harm each other or feeling overwhelmed, powerful mirror neurons in our brains fire and our brain/body response is to feel as if we ourselves are in danger. We are hardwired to feel this way at first and are jolted into action. Anger sometimes is a way we act before we can apply our higher-level reasoning to situations and react more calmly.

The goal is to be self-aware enough to know why we are angry and what primary emotions and fears underlie this anger. This will enable us to gain control through finding coping strategies that help us calm down in everything but the most dangerous situation. For example, it is helpful to use an attention-getting, sharp yelling voice when a child is about to run into the parking lot where she could potentially get hit by a car. However, using an angry voice that stops a child short every time she tries to dip her paintbrush in the yellow after using the blue would not be appropriate. In that situation, a teacher might reflect and say, "Wow, I am a neat freak because when I was growing up, my older sister was really protective of her art stuff and yelled at me for messing with it. This child, though, does not really understand that putting the paintbrush into the yellow after using the blue might dirty the paint. Instead of yelling at her like my sister did to me, I am going to show her that mixing the two colors will make green and show her how to wash the brush so she can keep her yellow paint yellow." In these examples, what might the primary emotion underlying the teacher's angry response be? Is it possible that in both cases, the teacher was scared? Certainly, it is obvious with the child running into the parking lot that the teacher was scared that she would get hit. In the second example, what might the teacher have been afraid of?

Unexpected or Surprising Anger

Anger can also be touched upon when we perceive that other people are getting something that we needed but did not get. We can recognize situations where supervisors or coworkers treat us differently, and this can either feel good, such as when we are seen for the individuals we are, or feel bad if we feel like we are not treated with respect or are being evaluated in an unfair way. This can stretch back into our own childhoods, too. It can even come into play when we watch our coworkers tending to children. If we have issues left over from our childhoods, such as having wanted more physical affection or more attention from our parents or caregivers, it can be very painful to watch others receiving affection or attention. It can even make us mad to have to give to children what we feel like we did not get. This can be emotionally charged and sometimes is hard to recognize.

Concept of Transference

Transference occurs when we react to another person as if he or she were someone else in our past or present, instead of seeing the person in front of us for who he or she really is (Berzoff et al. 2002). This may sound strange, but it happens a lot without us knowing it, and most of the time it is harmless. Think about how you might react to meeting a woman who reminds you of a grandmother who used to cook amazing food for you when you were little. You probably would instantly react positively toward the stranger because you felt this connection. This can be problematic, though, if, for example, a child reminds you of a kid in your neighborhood who used to tease you. It takes a lot of courage to explore those situations that caused us hurt in our own pasts. The more we can develop an awareness of such situations and see where the landmines of anger, jealousy, pain, sadness, shame, and fear lie, the more we can navigate without constantly stepping on them and getting trapped into situations where we feel out of control.

Sadness, joy, shame, and fear are all part of the human experience. The more painful emotions are hard to sit with, and joy can lift us to new heights. Floods of any emotion can color our judgment and cause us to react in a variety of ways, but usually we go about our lives with some predictable patterns. We might be sad when a loved one who has died is absent every Thanksgiving, but we might be happy when we look at photos of the good times had with him. Mixed feelings are something that can be confusing to us and that children have definitely not figured out by the time we work with them in preschool and early childcare settings. We are teaching them that being sad does not mean being depressed forever, that being angry does not mean that a relationship is destroyed, and that they do not have to feel ashamed of having feelings that are confusing. Sometimes, primary emotions were experienced so much during childhood that a variety of experiences trigger them, often without our awareness (Lieberman & Van Horn 2005). Trauma can literally change the way neurons in our brains communicate through chemical signals that cause them to fire (Perry et al. 1995). Our brains adapted so that we survived our individual childhoods, and part of this depended on how we were when we were born: genetics, what our experience was in utero, and so on. It is beyond the scope of this book to explore this exciting world of how nature and nurture came together to make possible the unique individuals we are right now, but let's just say that it involves a lot of complex and marvelous factors.

Know Thyself

Part of what makes us so marvelous is that we, as humans, are very resilient. What ties us together and helps support us to cope even in the darkest times of despair is a huge desire and drive to socially interact with others. Finding ways to talk to loved ones, coworkers, supervisors, and, yes, sometimes even the children we work with can be immensely helpful in healing old wounds, understanding our own reactions, and gaining insight into areas where we might need to put some attention. Have you ever had the experience of a friend zeroing in on something that might have taken you months to realize? That can happen in any area of life, and it certainly can happen often in early childcare and education settings when there is a whirlwind of many children, parents, coworkers, supervisors, inspectors, and others to contend with every day. Wouldn't we like to know where we can improve and be able to have a warm, supportive environment where we can explore our own challenges and intense feelings so that we can use these in our work with children? That is where safe, reflective supervision ties into developing self-awareness and security in using a relationship-based approach.

Reflective Supervision

Supervision is a delicate process. Your supervisor is responsible for guiding and evaluating your performance as an employee and often also functions as a director in the capacity of being responsible for maintaining the safety and well-being of all the children in care. Your relationship with your supervisor may be lovely and give you a much-needed break, or it can be stressful and can feel like running a gauntlet. We hope that this book inspires you to think about ways that you can use supervision to understand yourself and your work in an emotional and relationship-based framework. This involves feeling very safe in your relationship with your supervisor. This does not mean that your supervisor has to become your close friend or that you must share intimate personal details with your supervisor, but it does mean that you can strive to develop a working relationship based on who you and your supervisor are and your comfort levels with emotions that allow you to explore when something feels hard or stuck in the ways you relate to children. Feeling safe in relationships can be enhanced by consistency and feeling that you are a valued employee. After all, this is a job where satisfaction often has to come from how appreciated you feel and how much you love the work, rather than from earning a high salary.

Consistency Is the Key

Having a regular and consistent time to talk that allows enough time to relax and explore examples of times where you might need support or to explore your reactions is a key component to being able to effectively use supervision. Some of us are adept at spontaneously talking about our experiences, but some of us need time to get to the deeper emotions that might be at the root of our most profound challenges and that might be the key to finding our way to the best successes. Also, if a supervisor is trying to listen to you but also has ten other tasks waiting, you probably will not get the undivided attention needed to tune into helping you uncover what is going on and find a solution. If consistent, uninterrupted time with your supervisor is not built into your workplace routine, start advocating for it, and use this book to talk about how it could help the entire staff!

Reflective supervision goes beyond what most people think of as supervision. Key components of reflective supervision include the following:

- A safe environment where you can reflect on your relationships with children, colleagues, and supervisors without feeling judged or criticized
- Supervision from someone who has some distance to be able to offer guidance, feedback, and direction in a positive way
- Recognition that working with children and parents (especially those who might have been traumatized) arouses many feelings—including rescue fantasies, anger, hopelessness, and helplessness—that can be coped with and understood with support of the supervisor
- Nonjudgmental space to talk about the demands and pressures that can lead to burnout and to find flexible solutions to avoid secondary traumatization
- A space to tell about unusual reactions such as nightmares, headaches, stress responses, and so on to see if they are related to work or perhaps are signs of things outside work that are impacting your job and have a supervisor's support in thinking through how to reduce stress (van Horn and Lieberman 2008)

The Task of the Supervisor

In order to feel safe in talking about your relationships and feelings, you must feel that your supervisor supports your work and generally treats you with respect and a warm, positive regard. This means that your supervisor can show you that you are a trusted and valued employee. Your relationships with your coworkers can become competitive if you feel that they are getting this and you are not. Even more distressing, you cannot do your best work with emotionally intense children when you are plagued with doubts and insecurity about your work and whether you will be criticized at every turn. In order to get this trust and positive regard, you must also be ready to give it to those around you.

If you are not feeling trusted and respected, it is time to gather the courage to create an opportunity to explore, in a non-defensive way, what might be happening with your supervisor. You must be prepared to acknowledge your own strengths and weaknesses in a nondefensive manner, which raises feelings of vulnerability. If you think that you are doing your best work and your supervisor does not, it makes sense that you need to figure out why. First, you have to take stock of the concrete aspects of the job, such as whether you are able to be physically and emotionally safe with children, whether you are aware of the classroom dynamics and work well with others, whether you can promote an organized and clean space, whether you complete paperwork on time and arrive on time for work, and so on. You also have to troubleshoot in any areas that are hard for you. If you are certain that you are providing good service and adhering to the policies and job expectations, you can explore your and your supervisor's temperaments, personalities, communication styles, and cultural differences as possible areas of difference. Chances are if your supervisor hired you and keeps you on, he or she likes and values at least some aspects of your work; build on your strengths and accept your weaknesses by asking for help. Ask for permission to try new things and discuss the outcomes with your supervisor, or ask for more information.

Cultural Norms

Culture comes in many forms. We never inhabit just one culture, although we might strongly identify with a specific one. Cultures include the country in which you live; the neighborhood in which you grew up or currently live; the ethnic, racial, or linguistic traditions that shape your everyday world; your family's unique patterns of living and ways of communicating; your workplace's expectations for how you act; what language you speak; how you dress; and so on. Again, we see how complicated the world of our work is, especially when cultures may compete or be at odds with one another. If we're confused as to how to deal with differences in values in childrearing, most likely the children we serve are, too! Their parents may have reactions that we feel are either justified or surprising and maybe irritating, depending on how the culture of our childcare center or preschool syncs with the parents' own modes of being. It is important to take a step back and consider all of these factors as we interact with young children and their families.

Take a Nonjudgmental Stance

As with any relationship, if you can avoid judging and assuming from the outset and can connect in some way with parents and children, you can make positive changes in children's lives. Ask lots of questions. The more information you have and the more you can hear what a parent or child is saying, the more you can understand their perspective, their culture, their stress, and their motivation. If you want a parent to treat a child well, you can model how to do this by respecting the parent and use respectful questions to try to promote change. Many parents who struggle with parenting are facing many challenges in their lives, and they may not know how to change their disagreeable behaviors. We can help them understand why change is needed much more effectively if we understand why they use the parenting strategies they do and what they hope to accomplish.

When Safety Is a Concern

In extreme cases, we need the assistance of child protective services to help families be safe. It can be the most difficult and painful call you make, but as mandated reporters we have the duty to make the call to protective services when children are not safe. Although it is hard to talk about, we recommend that you find a private space to talk about this call with the parents prior to making it. The more you know about the process, the more you can emphasize how this is a process that will hopefully help the child and family get services they need so that the child can be safe from harm.

Staff Process and Team Building

Many of the same types of skills we discussed earlier in this chapter in the "Reflective Supervision" section also apply to relationships with coworkers and staff. Finding ways to understand each other, finding words to convey in respectful and nonjudgmental ways things that might be helpful to coworkers in their work, and problem solving can be essential to building a safe and supportive team environment. When you feel comfortable, supported, and safe with your staff team, the children in your care will feel secure. This is similar to children feeling secure at home when their parents are getting along with other adults in the house. When you talk through issues rather than avoid difficulties, you can often find common ground. Secrets can undermine the entire workplace and create stress that is scary because staff might sense that there is a potential threat to the work environment that we rely on for their livelihood. It is important to look at how to equalize the stress if one staff member seems to bear the brunt of it.

Scapegoating sometimes arises in groups. This is when one staff member is attacked and blamed for wrongdoings or mistakes. Or sometimes one feels that he or she does the same things that other coworkers do but gets a different response. Just as we help children who may be ostracized by others and bring them into the group we need to do the same for our coworkers. We need to be open to seeing our coworkers in new ways and have the courage to talk openly when misunderstandings arise. Supervisors who promote open dialogue can combat strain among team members. Connection with coworkers prevents insecurity, competitiveness, jealousy, burnout, and cliques that can undermine effective teamwork in the classroom. These kinds of connections take time, energy, and patience.

Administrative Staff Support

It is a delicate thing to ask for something from someone who has a lot on their plate at work, but we encourage you to use administrative support or to ask your supervisor for permission to talk to higher-ups if you have a good idea about how a work process or procedure could work better. We all like to feel valuable and useful. Often, if you staff ask for administrative support in a way that recognizes the good job that person is doing, he or she will be happy to help you. Giving back in small ways can make administrative staff feel a part of the important work that you do.

This Is Hard Work

Are you exhausted just thinking about exploring all these feelings and their roots and how to understand and communicate about them? That's exactly what we're talking about when we say that work with young children is emotional, exhilarating, and draining! Our goal is to help you gain the confidence to know that you are a work in progress, just like the children you serve. It is a wonderful thing in life that we keep learning and growing. Your life will change over time, you will gain confidence in your experience, and you will face new life and work challenges that can alter your expectations or affect how you cope.

References

Berzoff, Joan, Laura Melano Flanagan, and Patricia Hertz. 2002. *Inside Out and Outside In: Psychodynamic Clinical Theory and Practice in Contemporary Multicultural Contexts*. New Jersey: Jason Aronson, Inc.

Lieberman, Alicia F. and Patricia Van Horn. 2005. *Don't Hit My Mommy! A Manual for Child-Parent Psychotherapy with Young Witnesses of Family Violence*. Washington, DC: Zero to Three Press.

Lieberman, Alicia F. and Patricia Van Horn. 2008. *Psychotherapy with Infants and Young Children: Repairing the Effects of Stress and Trauma on Early Attachment.* New York: Guilford Press.

Perry. B. D., R. A. Pollard, T. L. Blakley, W. Baker, and D. Vigilante. "Childhood Trauma, the Neurobiology of Adaptation, and 'Use-dependent' Development of the Brain: How 'States' Become 'Traits.'" *Infant Mental Health Journal* 16 (Winter 1995). Pages 271-291

CHAPTER 7

Parents

Collaboration with parents is a very important part of your work caring for children. Children spend much of their time with their families, and these relationships are a significant driving force informing their personalities, ideas about the world, behavior, and expressions of emotion. The relationships you make with parents at the beginning of the school year will help you to get to know the children in Phase One, separate from them during Phase Two, and help them to make use of all they have learned in Phase Three.

Communication with Parents Is Key

You, your co-teachers, the director or principal, and the structure of your program will determine how you want to engage in communication with parents. You may want to send out weekly newsletters, schedule quarterly meetings, have informal check-ins at pick-up and drop-off, or host parent meetings at your school. Initially, your goal is to get to know the families and to know the children through the parent or caregiver's eyes. We recognize that in some situations, you may have very limited contact with parents. Providing a variety of opportunities for parental involvement will help ensure continuity of care. Parents are ultimately the experts on their own children, and often they can provide insight into difficult situations. For example, if a parent shares that his child did not sleep well the night before due to a thunderstorm, you will have a greater understanding about why the child might be clingier or louder

> **Collaboration with parents is a very important part of your work caring for children**

than usual throughout the day. Sharing information back and forth is an important way of getting to know children. This gives you a better sense of who the children are and allows you to meet their needs more effectively. Parents also find pleasure in knowing how their child's day went and what may be impacting the evening ahead. Children also find comfort in knowing that their teacher and their parent will share important information and hold them in mind; this promotes the trust and comfort that are key in Phase One.

As we discussed in previous chapters, the Relationship-Based Phase Model is built upon the idea that all behavior has meaning. This may be a new idea for parents, who are responding to their children's daily ups and downs with their own set of feelings and reactions. Often, teachers and parents need to work together to figure out why a child is displaying a particular behavior. Children cannot always communicate directly with words about their experience, but they surely will let you know by their action and emotional state that something is happening. You may need to be the one to let parents know that it is important to share information about big events, such as moving to a new house, or even small ones, such as the previous thunderstorm example. Parents themselves may not value sharing this information or may not realize that you as a teacher want to know about their children in this way. In fact, parents may not even be sold on the idea that behavior has meaning and may attribute behaviors to a child's inherent "badness." The following is an example:

Katie, age four, and other children in the classroom recently began to engage in teasing, leaving others out of group play, and other behavior that the classroom teachers decided to try to reduce. When the teacher talked to Katie's mom about her role in this classroom trend, Katie's mom said, "That's just how girls are. I had to deal with it all through high school."

In this instance, the teacher was providing the mother with information about recent classroom events and asking for her partnership in limiting it. Katie's mom appeared to feel that this was normal behavior, which provides the teacher with information about the norms and rules that may exist in Katie's home. This anecdote serves to show that this idea of collaboration does not always mean that parents and teachers come together with a shared idea. However, even this example of "failed" collaboration gives the teacher information about the parent's values, which can be useful moving forward with the child.

Trauma

The relationships you make with parents and the relationship you foster between parents are especially important when children experience trauma. For example, if there is a trauma experienced by the greater community, such as a shooting nearby or a natural disaster, parents will feel supported by your knowledge of the events and their understanding that their children will be supported in processing their emotional reactions to the event. For trauma within a family, such as the death of a sibling, ongoing collaboration becomes even more important. You may find yourself scheduling weekly phone calls with the parent to ensure that you have access to the latest information and to share about the child's progress in school. In these situations, having opened avenues of communication can help everyone find connection and support in the face of devastating situations.

Fostering Supportive Community Among Parents

Monthly parent meetings may be a nice place to start fostering community and communication among parents. Parents can learn about the classroom and what the children do on a daily basis. They can also get to know one another and ultimately find a place to gain support and encouragement in the often-difficult world of parenting. As their children's teacher, you can support parents in feeling that their children are similar to other children and in understanding the typical developmental tasks of same-age children. This may normalize for parents some of the more challenging aspects of the parent-child relationship.

CHAPTER 8

Relationship-Based Early Childhood Mental Health Consultation

> Consultation at early childhood education and care sites is often done by a mental health professional, such as a psychologist or social worker.

Consultation at early childhood education and care sites is often done by a mental health professional, such as a psychologist or social worker. The purpose of consultation is for your center or school to have support in thinking through how to promote the emotional, psychological, and social conditions for optimal development and functioning with peers and adults. This can take many forms and should be flexible enough to meet your site's needs.

Consultants first and foremost meet with directors and supervisors to get information on how they view things as functioning. Most of the time, consultants meet with a point person every time they come to make sure that they are working closely with and promoting the aims of the center in formulating recommendations and communicating with staff.

A consultant generally observes classrooms and staff meetings and makes supportive suggestions for how to promote emotional awareness, effective problem solving and communication, and classroom strategies and modifications to help children with difficulties or during times of the day that are generally hard for many children, such as transitions. The beauty of having a consultant is that this person is not a supervisor or director and can have a distance from the day-to-day problems that allows perspective to think of new suggestions. Consultants often have worked with families in mental health settings and can help with how to talk to parents about their children's difficulties. They can also offer resources to parents who are often fearful of what teachers will say or demand of them.

What Works for Consultation

Maintaining an open mind to what a consultant suggests is key to the relationship. Unless you feel that the consultant is very off base, try his or her new suggestions for a few weeks and see if they are helpful. Take your experiences back to the consultant and discuss what felt helpful about the experience and what might have felt hard about it. If you completely disagree with the suggestion, we encourage you to respectfully voice your concerns and say why you think the suggestion would not work or would be harmful. This allows a fuller discussion about the suggestion.

Consultants who go into classrooms to observe can be helpful in on-the-ground problem solving or for viewing the classroom as a whole and how all the staff and children interact. For example, one consultant shared this experience:

> *I went into Mr. Rob and Ms. Vivi's classroom, and the children were more or less engaged in their activities at different stations. Andre all of a sudden erupted into tears when Laya bossed him around in the house area by preventing him from touching all the food and pots and relegating him to being the baby. Mr. Rob went over to the doll corner and stood with his hands on his hips, and Laya smiled up at him. Andre continued crying. Ms. Vivi took a sideways look at Mr. Rob and left the classroom, going to the bathroom. Andre fled the space, and Mr. Rob used a sharp voice to stop him from running after Ms. Vivi.*

The consultant was able to talk with Mr. Rob and Ms. Vivi, along with their supervisor, about strategies for having more communication across the room between the teachers to help the children feel safe and contained. The consultant offered suggestions for them about how they could subgroup the classroom and communicate between the groups, including informing each other and giving the children warning when one left the space. This led to a wider discussion of how Ms. Vivi felt that Mr. Rob was placed as lead teacher over her because he was a man, and the supervisor was able to talk about why this decision was made. Even though this did not resolve the problem, the consultant felt that she was able to provide a space where a safe dialogue could happen around issues that were clearly affecting this team of teachers.

Consultants often face limitations in the numbers of hours they are at sites, so communication is key to consultants' using the time they have effectively. Consultants often can be supportive listeners and effective in helping to problem-solve with directors, who are usually alone in their responsibility to make important choices that might sometimes involve painful decisions about priorities. Since consultants are outside the system, directors sometimes feel that consultants can be helpful in addressing concerns or identifying priorities.

When to Refer Out

There is an art to making referrals. Often, we are afraid that parents will reject our referrals or will blame us for the things we worry about in the classroom. Whether a child is in distress a lot of the time or painfully shy, using aggression to an alarming degree, having communication problems, having a lot of difficulty playing at age level with peers, or seems as if he or she is having a hard time physically navigating the classroom environment or playing, we cannot ignore that child's distress signs.

Often, if children get help in the early years, they avoid problems in the future, when the expectations on them will be higher and risks of school failure greater. Sometimes, a child's signs of distress can reveal serious problems at home, making talking about the problems with parents or caregivers more difficult. As much as possible, you should make a referral in a positive way, emphasizing the desire to understand and help the child and family. Be clear about what you have tried to do in the classroom and why you think it is not enough. Give the parents or caregivers time and space to talk about their understanding of their child's difficulties and enlist them as an ally in promoting their child's wellbeing.

If the situation is becoming unsafe, physically or emotionally, for others, teachers sometimes make getting help outside the classroom a necessary step to keep a child in the program. Consultants can offer resources for services in your area and often can help talk to parents about the services and what it will be like for them and their children to get extra help.

When a Child's Needs Cannot Be Met

Asking a child to leave a program can involve a range of feelings, including sadness about the good-bye; feelings of relief that the stress of keeping a child in a program where he or she is struggling greatly is over; and disappointment or feelings of failure at not having been able to help or rescue a child in distress. However, a child who regularly puts him- or herself or other children at risk (physically or emotionally) and whose parents and caregivers are not able to get him or her the help needed to become more emotionally and physically regulated will not feel safe in your program and will not be able to learn and grow to his or her potential.

When we remember that all behavior has meaning, if a child is in constant distress or frequently is outside the group, he or she is not benefiting from what your program has to offer. Forming an alliance with parents and caregivers in deciding when a child should leave the program can be difficult, but the above strategy of trying to enlist the parent as a partner in figuring out what a child needs is all the more important when deciding that a child is inappropriate for your setting. In some areas, there are programs where children with more intense needs can get more individualized or small-group attention. Consultants can be helpful in gathering resources and talking to parents so that you do not feel as if a parent or caregiver is leaving empty-handed and without support.

Family Counseling

Family counseling can help parents and caregivers understand what their children need. Although family counseling is a time and resource commitment for families, often it can be a good place to start to get a child help, especially if the child seems to be having strong emotional reactions and intense distress or painful shyness. Young children need their caregivers to be part of their healing and to be able to talk about their life experiences. Families often learn that play is the child's most natural language and that with the help of a trained therapist, they can connect with a child to understand what his or her is communicating through difficult or worrisome behavior. Another great thing about family counseling is that parents and caregivers can also find hope of getting help with some of their own emotional and social difficulties.

Understanding/Communicating with Related Fields

Children who are receiving mental health counseling such as family counseling or behavioral therapy, speech therapy, occupational therapy to help with tasks such as writing and to address sensory integration difficulties, physical therapy, and other types of services can benefit from your collaboration with other professionals. As the school year starts, it can be helpful to ask all parents whether children are receiving services and to voice that you would be open to talking to these outside professionals. Occasionally, being open to having a conversation about a child on the phone or having a therapist visit to see the child in the school environment can help all involved understand how to best intervene to help the child.

CHAPTER 9

Frequently Asked Questions

1. Why is social-emotional content integral to early childhood education?

Human beings' first "learning" is within the context of relationships. Learning how to be with and relate to others happens first within the family and then moves outward to include extended family members and early childhood teachers and peers. Thus the "teaching" begins at home with early attachment relationships and then continues with teachers. Children need to feel emotionally secure and to know that their needs are going to be met in order to settle into the classroom for learning.

2. How and when do I refer for services?

You should consider making a referral for family therapy or child assessment when a child is clearly having daily challenges in areas of separating, transitioning, sharing, waiting, playing next to peers, using language when he or she is frustrated, and hitting peers or teachers. Of course this is done with the parents after having kept the parents in the loop as to the challenges the child is displaying. This should be done a month to a month and a half *after* the child's entry into your program. Referral making is individual, as many children display various challenges when first beginning preschool, but depending on what is transpiring in the home, the time of adjustment can lengthen. Life events that may affect a child's behavior include a recent family move, birth of a sibling, parental separation or death, or parental job loss. These types of big changes can result in temporary behavior changes in children, but it is recommended that you refer families to outside support if the problematic behaviors persist. Sometimes if you see a child who appears to be especially sensitive to light, sound, or touch, you might want to consider an occupational therapy referral to rule out sensory integration challenges. If a child's speech and language production seems to be less than his or her peers, a referral for a speech and language assessment is in order.

3. When should I consider sub-grouping?

Subgrouping works well when you have a group of fifteen or more children who are predominantly three-year-olds or three- and four-year-olds who are having their first school experience and thus are challenged to wait during circle time activities. Also if the subgroups have the same teacher for a lengthy period of time, especially at the school year's beginning, subgrouping allows for easier attachment and integration into the classroom experience as a whole.

4. How do I make individual plans for children? What about the rest of the group?

You might consider implementing an individual plan when you notice that a particular child might benefit from a more direct, literally hands-on experience. Individual plans can be initiated at various times, including circle time, when a seat next to you might benefit an especially fidgety child; moving to line up, when a hand on the shoulder might be helpful; or prior to a transition, when a special/private invitation might be called for. For the most part children are less worried about a peer having a special plan than adults are. If the adults see the benefit of addressing individual needs in the context of a group, they should say with confidence, "This is what so-and-so needs right now. If or when you require something extra, we will provide that for you."

5. How do I engage parents in a meaningful way?

Engaging parents begins when you first meet them, hopefully prior to the start of the school year. At drop-off time, make sure to look at parents and greet them first. You will be with their child during class time so acknowledgment of the child can wait. Should you want to share information specific to their child, make a time outside of class for private discussions. Sharing information at drop-off or pick-up is not productive and only serves to heighten anxiety. A simple, "Let's make a time to get together" shows respect for all. When you have developed this kind of respectful relationship with parents, it becomes much easier to do things such as make referrals to outside services.

6. How do I explain social-emotional content to parents?

In order for parents to "buy what you're selling," you have to believe it yourself. By this we mean that you should only explain to parents aspects of social-emotional development that you yourself understand and embrace. Emotional intelligence paves the way for later learning, so you can explain to parents that social-emotional goals in preschool allow children to be more successful students, friends, and human beings. Attributes such as being able to read social cues, waiting and attending, and understanding others' emotions are part and parcel of social-emotional development. Reminding parents about child development and what behaviors are developmentally appropriate can also help them to adjust expectations for their children.

7. How does *Connections: The Relationship-Based Phase Model* mesh with Reggio, GOLD, and other early childhood curriculums?

Connections: The Relationship-Based Phase Model is a model for thinking about your relationships with the children in your care. It can be integrated into most, if not all, preschool curriculums without disrupting your educational goals. Some aspects of Phase One, such as giving children individual set-ups for play materials or refraining from giving classroom jobs, may feel disruptive to your natural way of operating your classroom. Even though this may be a significant shift for teachers, the classroom curriculum generally does not prohibit it. Ultimately, when children have a secure relationship with their teachers, they can begin to take on these independent roles later in the school year, with much more success than if they are given these daunting tasks too soon.

8. Why is it important that I encourage my staff to use *Connections: The Relationship-Based Phase Model* in making their lesson plans?

This model is a helpful way to think about the progression of a typical classroom year. It provides a structure for thinking about how to meet children's social-emotional needs. It can be particularly validating for teachers to

Connections: The Relationship-Based Phase Model is a model for thinking about your relationships with the children in your care.

know that behaviors during these phases are typical and normal and not manipulative or needy. This can allow teachers to have more empathy for their students. The activities, songs, and books for each phase help children to communicate their emotions, which can be validating for the children and also helps teachers to understand the children's needs better. Using *Connections: The Relationship-Based Phase Model* while making lesson plans helps ensure that teachers incorporate the model into their classroom.

9. What's the best way for me to encourage reluctant staff to use the *Connections: The Relationship-Based Phase Model*?

Directors need to "buy it" if they are going to try to "sell it" to staff. If staff is reluctant, we recommend encouraging them to try the model for the school year to see how it feels. More often than not, staff will fall in love with it and will find that their students are more regulated, calm, emotionally expressive, and capable of learning new things.

10. What do I do if I suspect abuse or neglect?

If teachers routinely witness disturbing or overly harsh interactions between parents and children, or if a child reveals information about neglectful or abusive parenting, teachers are mandated by law to report this information to local Child Protective Services. *Any* marks such as bruises, welts, burns, and so on caused by a parent or caregiver, even if caused by a seemingly benign spanking, *must be reported*. Sexualized behaviors from a child such as frequent masturbation, talking about topics that are inappropriate for the age group, preoccupation with sex or body parts, and sexualized play with toys or peers are all red flags. These behaviors may be a sign of anxiety but should be investigated by Child Protective Services in order to make sure children are safe. It goes without saying that if a child is in immediate danger, you should call 911. Your job as a teacher is not to determine whether abuse or neglect occurred but to alert the appropriate authorities who are trained to do these types of investigations in order to help the child and the parents. Your center director should have the phone number for your local Child Protection agency, but generally you can find this information online if you search your state's name and "child protective services." Often, we recommend alerting parents that you will be making this phone call, and it is always preferable to call with the parents present so they know what you are reporting to authorities.

CHAPTER 10

Theoretical Underpinnings

Preschool is a busy intersection of play-based learning, new relationships with adults outside the family, an expanded peer network, new routines, saying good-bye to parents for extended periods of time, and more. Teachers have long recognized the importance of a good start for children from an early age, and exciting research is being done in far-reaching fields to inform and support teachers in providing optimal care and education. Research in many fields, including education, child development, social work, psychology, biology, neuroscience, occupational therapy, medicine, history, and more, inform the work in this book. The basic theoretical underpinning that *Connections: The Relationship-Based Phase Model* rests upon is that a secure attachments between young children and caregivers promote the social and emotional foundations for learning in the preschool years.

> *The Relationship-Based Phase Model* rests upon is that a secure attachments between young children and caregivers promote the social and emotional foundations for learning in the preschool years.

The Mental Health Context: Research on Attachment and Early Caregiving Experiences

Children are born with temperaments that influence their approaches to new situations, and early secure relationships with attuned caregivers are pivotal in helping children develop a trust in the world that will influence relationships in the future (Stern 1973, 192). Children whose parents or caregivers are able to relate to and help them emotionally regulate by supporting a manageable level of frustration without overwhelming a child generally are shown to be more able by preschool age to feel secure in new relationships, as they are confident that their worlds are safe and that basic needs will be met in a reasonable amount of time without the child becoming distressed. Siegel and Hartzell state, "Emotion as a fundamental integrating process is an aspect of virtually every function of the human brain" (2003, 59). In their view, human emotions take a lot of bits of information from inside the child and the outer world and tie them together into a meaningful whole picture. Before a baby, toddler, or preschooler can use emotion to form a coherent picture that matches the reality of a situation fairly well, a caregiver must be able to do this with the child to help him or her gradually build the capacity to do this by him- or herself. A trauma-informed approach to viewing children shows that children who have more security in their attachments to important caregivers and more safety in their homes generally are more flexible and resilient in their approaches to new people, situations, and demands and are more comfortable in exploring. Children who have secure attachments are generally shown to have better outcomes in life. This is why this book was written—to connect the mental health research with the research on positive school outcomes!

Connections: The Relationship-Based Phase Model started with modest roots in Winnicott's theory of a "holding environment."

Brain and nervous system research has taken off in the past few decades, with greater technology and a range of techniques for observing and analyzing human behavior, emotions, cognitive functions, chemical reactions and messages among systems inside the human body, communication between humans, and more. The scientific resources are vast and are informed by animal and human studies. *Connections: The Relationship-Based Phase Model* started with modest roots in Winnicott's theory of a "holding environment." He talks about how young children need to be in a relationship with "good enough" caregivers who are reasonably able to keep them safe, secure, and attuned to in order to develop from a state of dependency toward more independence (Winnicott 1960). We view the classroom as an opportunity to create an environment where children can feel "held" in emotional, psychological, and physical ways in order to have the energy and resources to learn.

Much of this book ties together what therapists do with children and families children's psychological, emotional, and relational health. Shedler relates that the key elements to promoting mental health using

Psychodynamic Therapy are focus on emotional expression, exploration of attempts to avoid distressing feelings and thoughts, looking for patterns and themes, talking about the past, focusing on relationships, and exploring fantasy life (2010, 99). When we reflect on this list, we can see the relationship between these therapy tools and the tools that attuned preschool teachers use with children to help children connect to what is important to them, navigate a variety of peer relationships, and relate in positive ways to authority figures and caregivers. We can also see what things provoke a range of positive and negative emotions for children.

Humans rarely survive in isolation, and much research has been done on various types of groups in a many fields. Through research in communities and types of situations where different groups come together and interact, stages of group development have been identified and studied. The concept that groups go through stages that allow group members to gain a sense of belonging, learn about social relationships, fulfill roles in the group context, test authority, manage emotions in the presence of others, and ultimately become relatively able to function independently has been written extensively about by Irvin Yalom and others (Yalom 1995). Groups are interconnected, and in this book we talk about group development in terms of children in a classroom, but we invite you to think about how all the groups in your life are numerous and overlapping. It often is useful to reflect on how experience in families often is reflected in how the children—and we—are in groups.

Culture and Context

A family's culture, language, and context shape the ways that children come to experience their world. Rogoff talks about the importance of viewing children as participants in "dynamically related cultural communities," rather than as having a box to check on a form asking for a category such as race, language, or ethnicity (2003, 77). In viewing children as having the capacity to shift among different communities and roles, we see that they are generally very good at understanding their place in a variety of cultures and will adapt to new situations if given help in understanding the new expectations and unwritten customs, values, and rules. Preschoolers are interested in and open to exploring similarities and differences in the wider world, and bring their curiosity to developing friendships. Rewards for children in connecting to community, customs and identity, and family traditions can come in the form of praise, privileges, and pride. A child's ways of relating, finding comfort and a sense of belonging, identity development, expressing emotions and thoughts, playing, and more are all deeply connected to his or her culture and experiences in early life. A child may encounter preschool, with its own cultural norms and values, as being very similar to those he or she experienced at home or very different. We have talked in previous chapters about the importance of bridging through a relationship with a child's caregivers as a way to help children whose cultural context at home and at school differ. Culture and experiences of similarity and difference play a huge part in preschool-aged children's comfort, security, and competence when entering a school setting. Diversity can be a result of a child growing up in a household where the culture, language, and customs are very different from your school setting, or where the differences may be more subtle. We believe that children who have a chance to be heard and are given space to share their own experience in a safe and supportive context can bridge the differences and gain comfort in similarities. Children with special needs (including children with trauma histories) often exhibit more challenges when faced with coping with the increased demands of navigating a cultural context that is very different from their own. Preschool classroom teachers can promote a sharing of ideas, languages, culture, and traditions through open dialogue and play (Lieberman and Van Horn 2008).

Child Development and the Positive Effects of Early Intervention and Developmentally Attuned Preschool Programs

The field of child development incorporates the physical, social, emotional, linguistic, cognitive, cultural, relational, and contextual realities of childhood. From a developmental viewpoint, children are unique individuals who have their own time frames and styles of completing developmental tasks. Children will meet milestones, but also will circle back to earlier modes of doing things, such as regressing in toileting and sucking their thumb when their mom has a new baby. However, we know that development for most children proceeds in the direction of gaining mastery over their own bodies, emotions, and skills needed for competence in adulthood. Research on child development necessarily incorporates the work of a wide range of professionals from far-flung fields, such as special education teachers, neuroscientists, pediatricians, social workers, psychologists, teachers, occupational therapists, speech therapists, and more. We often hear of a "developmental approach" to teaching, and the National Association for the Education of Young Children (NAEYC) disseminates much information on this approach. NAEYC provides accreditation and guidelines for creating a developmentally appropriate preschool setting.

The developmental approach aims to provide the experiences for learning and growing that allow children to progress in all domains of development without being overwhelmed. The developmental approach to teaching also incorporates room for individualizing a curriculum according to a child's individual needs, rather than requiring that all children be engaged in the same tasks at the same levels. This approach assumes that teachers are able to attune to children's needs and help them meet the next challenge in a way that respects their integrity and emotional wellbeing. Teachers are often asked to provide opportunities for young children to explore their own interests and engage in play in creative ways that promote natural interests and skills to solve problems through imaginative play (Davies 1999). The field of child development recognizes that preschool-aged children are naturals at learning and have curiosity to interact with the world and other people.

In 1986, the United States Congress established the Early Intervention program to provide services for infants and toddlers to help children develop and grow without the need later on for intensive services such as special education, institutionalization, medical services, and therapies (NICHY 2013). Early Intervention is based on the premise that children who experience developmentally appropriate care and education early in life tend to have better outcomes later in life. In addition, Early Intervention often involves parents and caregivers in children's therapy. Education research has shown that parent and family involvement often promotes children's success in school (Gates Foundation 2009). We are pleased to see preschool curricula proliferating that include the social and emotional dimensions of young children's experience and hope to further that through the *Connections: The Relationship-Based Phase Model*.

Professional Development

Our role in promoting the education, protection, and development of young children is invaluable, in theory, and research has shown that children who receive high-quality educational and Early Intervention programs have better chances later in life. Solid research show that putting money toward early childhood programs pays off in the long run by reducing the need for later job training and remedial education (Tough 2012). However, many professionals who work with young children as preschool teachers feel that the high value our society places on work with young children does not usually translate into being paid well and a sense of high professional esteem. We encourage professional preschool teachers to educate themselves and others and to speak up about children's needs, the importance of this work, and the value it should have in our society. Too often, people who speak for children are far away from the day-to-day world of children. We are the voices for these little ones who cannot speak for themselves.

Further Reading

We have included in our "References and Further Reading" section at the end of this book resources that range from articles and books that are geared toward an academic audience to materials that are designed to be read by a wider readership. Some of these books offer resources for specific topics that might be useful to your staff or to recommend to a parent. At our center, we have a bookshelf that houses books on a variety of topics that parents are free to borrow.

References

Davies, D. 1990. *Child Development: A Practitioner's Guide.* New York: Guildford Press.

Gates Foundation Report. 2009. Accessed December 30, 2013. http://www.gatesfoundation.org.

Lieberman, A. and P. Van Horn. 2008. *Psychotherapy with Infants and Young Children: Repairing the Effects of Stress and Trauma on Early Attachment.* New York: Guilford Press.

National Dissemination Center for Children with Disabilities. 2013. Accessed December 30. http://www.nichcy.org.

Rogoff, B. 2003. *The Cultural Nature of Human Development.* New York: Oxford University Press.

Seigel, D. and M. Hartzell. 2003. *Parenting From the Inside Out: How a Deeper Self-understanding Can Help You Raise Children Who Thrive.* New York: Penguin Putnam, Inc.

Shedler, J. "The Efficacy of Psychodynamic Psychotherapy." *American Psychiatrist*, 65(2) (February–March 2010).

Tough, P. 2012. *How Children Succeed*. New York: Houghton Mifflin Harcourt.

Winnicott, D. W. "The Theory of Parent-Infant Relationship." *The International Journal of Psychoanalysis* no. 41 (1960): 585–95.

Yalom, I. 1995. *The Theory and Practice of Group Therapy*. New York: Basic Books.

EPILOGUE

The Virginia Frank Child Development Center was inspired by Virginia Frank, who began her career in social work and social welfare in Chicago in 1911 as a caseworker with the Jewish Family Service Bureau. Virginia was born in 1890 in Germany and came to Chicago, where she was the director of Jewish Family and Community Services (now Jewish Child and Family Services). She worked at the agency for forty-four years. Virginia was trained in Europe and had experience in child psychotherapy. During her career she worked closely with colleagues Jane Addams and Julia Lathrop, iconic figures in Chicago's social work community. She was committed to the idea of providing mental health services for young children, an idea almost unheard of in the United States at that time. Virginia envisioned a therapeutic center where children who were deeply affected by trauma and loss in the aftermath of World War II and the Holocaust could heal and grow. The Virginia Frank Child Development Center became a reality in 1955.

The Center continues to provide family therapy and child therapy, as well as an intensive group therapy for young children called Therapeutic Nursery. Therapeutic Nursery provides daily group psychotherapy for small groups of children ages two- to six-years-old. The theoretical framework for these groups was and continues to be rooted in Attachment Theory, a psychological theory based on examining the beginning relationships between children and their primary caregivers (Karen 1994). Attachment theorists posited, and research has confirmed, that physiological and optimal developmental changes occur when a child is securely bonded with a primary caregiver (Seigel and Hartzell 2003). Children who have experienced physical or emotional trauma within the context of their early attachments can exhibit developmental and/or psychological challenges. Examples of this trauma can include death of a parent or sibling; injury or illness, including parental mental illness; or a significant mis-attunement with a primary caregiver (Lieberman and Van Horn 2008). Some attachment theorists suggest that children can repeat early stages of development within a supportive, therapeutic relationship and alter their developmental trajectory

(Cozolino 2010). In providing therapy, the staff at the Virginia Frank Child Development Center use this theoretical orientation to attend to the various aspects of healthy relationships. The Relationship-Based Phase Model has emerged out of the work of the daily program. It notes how over time, within the relationships formed in the therapy groups and at different stages of the year, children grow, heal, and change. The attachment perspective believes in the healing nature of relationships. Developmental issues are not hard-wired but can change within a caring relationship and safe environment.

As a teacher, you have surely witnessed children's incredible capacity for growth in the classroom. Your role in the lives of the children you are charged with is very important in this process. Teachers are also great resources for parents who may be struggling with their children at a certain phase in development. The relationship between you and the parents of the children that you care for can be a vital tool in promoting secure social-emotional development. What we know in our work is that children who aren't secure in their attachments have poor social-emotional skills. A child with poor social-emotional skills might misbehave and can be overwhelmed, anxious, and unfocused; these all-consuming emotions make the child unavailable for the learning tasks required of his or her age (Kaiser and Rasminsky 2003).

When we see children with this kind of presentation, they have often been referred to us from schools like yours where they have failed in a regular classroom setting. Our Therapeutic Nursery program allows these children to redo early social-emotional issues within their attachment to a primary therapist. That is why our work always begins with the family, the primary attachment figures for any child. The social worker who initially meets with the family will evaluate the family's difficulties and needs over time. We pay close attention to how the family interacts with each other and with us. Through sensitivity and responsiveness to the developmental needs of each family, we begin the process of working with them and helping them to feel comfortable at the Child Development Center. We know that the relationship between a parent and child is the most important of all relationships (Harwood, Miller and Irizarry 1995). We do not want to disrupt or threaten this relationship, but we work to facilitate it. We know that before a child can successfully separate from his or her parent and make use of people in the external world, he or she needs a solid foundation and a sense of predictability in the relationship (Emde 1989).

You may not see children who are so severely impacted by disrupted or insecure attachments. However, you might recognize some of the behaviors and anxieties that all children (and many adults!) exhibit in new and unfamiliar settings and relationships. For example, children will react when they are worried about being away from their parents, learning how to share, or learning about using the toilet. The Relationship-Based Phase Model gives you a tool kit for understanding and working with these typical developmental challenges.

The Virginia Frank Child Development Center staff has been providing mental health consultation to schools, Head Start centers, daycare centers, and home-based caregivers for as long as it has been in existence. We use the Relationship-Based Phase Model as a way to understand children's behaviors in groups over time. We teach it to directors, teachers, and caregivers to help them structure their programs and deepen their understanding of children's social-emotional development. Our model has been found to work with a variety of existing curricula, and many early childhood professionals with whom we have developed a relationship speak to the effectiveness of using our framework. Over the course of many years, directors of programs have asked, "Do you have a book about the Phase Model?" We are happy to say, "We do now!"

References

Cozolino, L. J. 2010. *The Neuroscience of Psychotherapy: Healing the Social Brain*. New York: W.W. Norton & Co.

Emde, R. N. 1989. "The Infant's Relationship Experience: Developmental and Affective Aspects." In *Relationship Disturbances in Early Childhood: A Developmental Approach*, edited by A. Sameroff and R. Emde, 33–51. New York: Basic Books.

Harwood, R. L., J. G. Miller, and N. L. Irizarry. 1995. *Culture and Attachment: Perceptions of the Child in Context*. New York: Guilford Press.

Kaiser, Barbara and Judy Sklar Rasminsky. 2003. *Challenging Behavior in Young Children: Understanding, Preventing, and Responding Effectively.* Boston: Pearson Education, Inc.

Karen, Robert. 1994. *Becoming Attached: First Relationships and How They Shape Our Capacity to Love.* New York: Oxford University Press.

Lieberman, Alicia F. and Patricia Van Horn. 2008. *Psychotherapy with Infants and Young Children: Repairing the Effects of Stress and Trauma on Early Attachment.* New York: Guilford Press.

Siegel, D. J., and M. Hartzell. 2003. *Parenting From the Inside Out: How a Deeper Self-understanding Can Help You Raise Children Who Thrive.* New York: J.P. Tarcher/Putnam.

Stern, D. N. 1985. *The Interpersonal World of the Infant: A View from Psychoanalysis and Developmental Psychology.* New York: Basic Books.

REFERENCES AND FURTHER READING

Atwool, N. 1997. "Attachment as a Context for Development: Challenges and Issues." *Children's Issues Seminar.* University of Otago, New Zealand.

Balaban, N. 2006. *Everyday Goodbyes.* New York: Teachers College Press.

Berzoff, J., L. Melano Flanagan, and P. Hertz. 2002. *Inside Out and Outside In: Psychodynamic Clinical Theory and Practice in Contemporary Multicultural Contexts.* New Jersey: Jason Aronson, Inc.

Cherry, C. 1996. *Parents, Please Don't Sit On Your Kids: A Parent's Guide to Nonpunitive Discipline.* Torrance, CA: Fearon Teacher Aids.

Cozolino, L. J. 2010. *The Neuroscience of Psychotherapy: Healing the Social Brain.* New York: W.W. Norton & Co.

Davies, D. 1999. *Child Development: A Practitioner's Guide.* New York: Guilford Press.

Elkind, D. 2001. *The Hurried Child.* Cambridge, MA: Da Capo Press.

Emde, R. N. 1989. "The Infant's Relationship Experience: Developmental and Affective Aspects." In *Relationship Disturbances in Early Childhood: A Developmental Approach*, edited by A. Sameroff and R. Emde, 33–51. New York: Basic Books.

Erikson, E. H. 1963. *Childhood and Society.* New York: Norton.

Gates Foundation Report. 2009. Accessed December 30, 2013. http://www.gatesfoundation.org.

Goldman, M. J. 2000. *The Joy of Fatherhood.* New York: Three Rivers Press.

Goldstein, E. 1995. *Ego Psychology and Social Work Practice.* New York: The Free Press.

Greenspan, S., and N. Lewis. 2000. *Building Healthy Minds: The Six Experiences that Create Intelligence and Emotional Growth in Babies and Young Children.* Boston: Da Capo Press.

Harding, C. G. 2007. *Begin with a Baby's Laughter and Other Essays on Infant Mental Health.* Chicago: Illinois Association for Infant Mental Health.

Harwood, R. L., J. G. Miller, and N. L. Irizarry. 1995. *Culture and Attachment: Perceptions of the Child in Context.* New York: Guilford Press.

Heroman, C., T. Bickart, and K. Berke. 2010. *Teaching Strategies GOLD: Objectives for Development and Learning.* Bethesda, MD: Teaching Strategies.

Karen, R. 1994. *Becoming Attached: First Relationships and How They Shape Our Capacity to Love.* New York: Oxford University Press.

Kaiser, B. and J. Rasminsky. 2003. *Challenging Behavior in Young Children: Understanding, Preventing, and Responding Effectively.* Boston: Pearson Education, Inc.

Koplow, L. 1996. *Unsmiling Faces: How Preschools Can Heal.* New York: Teachers College Press.

Kriete, R. 1999. *The Morning Meeting Book.* Turner Falls, MA: Northeast Foundation for Children Inc.

Kroen, W. C. 1996. *Helping Children Cope with the Loss of a Loved One.* Minneapolis: Free Spirit Publishing.

Kushner, H. S. 1981. *When Bad Things Happen to Good People.* New York: Anchor Books.

Levine, M. 1993. *All Kinds of Minds: A Young Student's Book about Learning Abilities and Learning Disorders.* Toronto: Educators Publishing Service, Inc.

Lieberman, A. F., and P. Van Horn. 2005. *Don't Hit My Mommy! A Manual for Child-Parent Psychotherapy with Young Witnesses of Family Violence.* Washington, DC: Zero to Three Press.

Lieberman, A. F. 1993. *The Emotional Life of the Toddler.* New York: Free Press.

Lieberman, A. F., and P. Van Horn (2008). *Psychotherapy with Infants and Young Children: Repairing the Effects of Stress and Trauma on Early Attachment.* New York: Guilford Press.

The National Center for Learning Disabilities. 2013. Accessed December 26. http://www.ncld.org/.

National Dissemination Center for Children with Disabilities. 2013. Accessed December 30. http://www.nichcy.org.

Perry. B. D., R. A. Pollard, T. L. Blakley, W. Baker, and D. Vigilante. "Childhood Trauma, the Neurobiology of Adaptation, and 'Use-dependent' Development of the Brain: How 'States' Become 'Traits.'" *Infant Mental Health Journal* 16 (Winter 1995). Pages 271-291

Rogoff, B. 2003. *The Cultural Nature of Human Development.* New York: Oxford University Press.

Sameroff, A., and R. Emde, Eds. 1989. *Relationship Disturbances in Early Childhood: A Developmental Approach.* New York: Basic Books.

Shedler, J. "The Efficacy of Psychodynamic Psychotherapy." *American Psychiatrist,* 65(2) (February–March 2010): 98–109.

Siegel, D. J., and M. Hartzell. 2003. *Parenting From the Inside Out: How a Deeper Self-understanding Can Help You Raise Children Who Thrive.* New York: J.P. Tarcher/Putnam.

Stern, D. 1985. *The Interpersonal World of the Infant: A View from Psychoanalysis and Developmental Psychology.* New York: Basic Books.

Tough, P. 2012. *How Children Succeed: Grit, Curiosity, and the Hidden Power of Character.* New York: Houghton Mifflin Harcourt.

Turecki, S., and L. Tonner. 1985. *The Difficult Child*. New York: Bantam Books.

Winnicott, D. W. 1958. *Collected Papers: Through Paediatrics to Psychoanalysis*. New York: Basic Books.

Winnicott, D. W. 1965. *The Maturational Processes and the Facilitating Environment*. London: Karnac.

Winnicott, D. W. "The Theory of Parent-Infant Relationship." *The International Journal of Psychoanalysis* no. 41 (1960): 585–95.

Yalom, I. 1995. *The Theory and Practice of Group Therapy*. New York: Basic Books.

ACKNOWLEDGMENTS

The authors are most grateful to the Boeing Employees Foundation for their generous support in helping us publish this manual. Thank you for your funds, encouragement, and patience. Many thanks to the Irving B. Harris Foundation and to the Prince Foundation for your generosity in supporting our Early Childhood Mental Health Program over many years. Your commitment to relationship-based clinical work is inspiring.

Our deep gratitude to Patrick Garnett, the office manager of the Virginia Frank Child Development Center, and to Coya Castro, our administrative assistant, for your computer skills, good humor, and great common sense.

Special thanks to proof-readers Elana Benatar, MA, LCSW who helped us begin this project and to Whitney Sullivan, LCSW. You read the manuscript with a critical eye and gave us useful feedback. We are grateful to Mollie Reed, M.Ed. for her expertise, wisdom, and advice.

Thanks to David Sisk, LCSW, an artist in all he does, for his cover design.

Thanks to Jewish Child and Family Services' CEO Howard Sitron, COO Margaret Vimont, and CFO Vincent Everson. Your support and help with the business aspects of this project were vital. Thank you to program supervisor Elizabeth Wyman and Barbara Chandler for being our "cheerleaders."

Our gratitude goes to the Albany Park Community Center Head Start program, especially to Dina Evans, Eva Volin, Ms. Adelina, and Ms. Hanka. Their willingness to open their classrooms to our funders and to try morning check-in was invaluable to this endeavor.

Finally, and most importantly, our sincere thanks to the staff of The Virginia Frank Child Development Center of Jewish Child and Family Services of Metropolitan Chicago both past and present. We stand on the shoulders of those who came before us and who always believed in the healing power of healthy relationships.

Made in the USA
Lexington, KY
01 July 2014